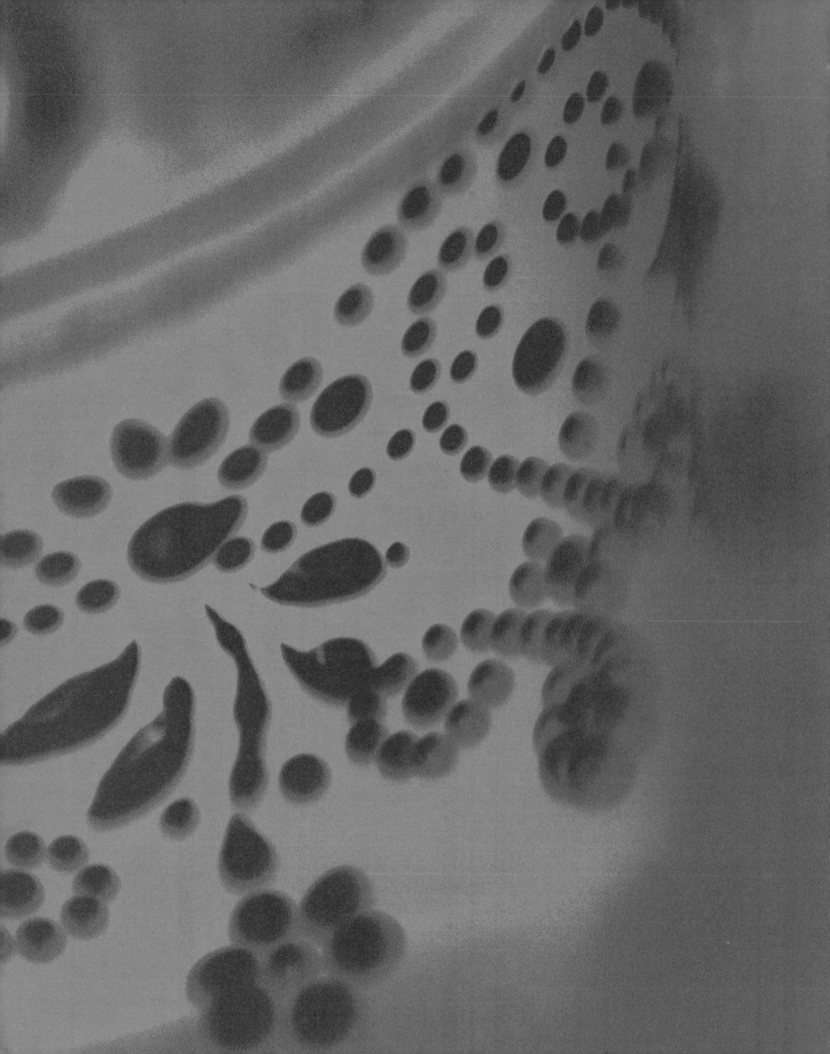

the
moroccan
collection

hamlyn

Publishing Director: Laura Bamford

Commissioning Editor: Nicola Hill
Editors: Sarah Ford and Anne Crane

Creative Director: Keith Martin
Senior Designer: Geoff Borin

Photographer: David Loftus
Home Economist: Fran Warde
Stylist: Antonia Gaunt
Indexer: Hilary Bird

Production Controller: Bonnie Ashby

The Moroccan Collection - Traditional Flavours from Northern Africa
Hilaire Walden
First published in 1998 by Hamlyn an imprint of Reed Consumer Books
Limited, Michelin House, 81 Fulham Road, London SW3 6RB
and Auckland, Melbourne, Singapore and Toronto

Copyright © 1998 Reed Consumer Books Limited

British Library Cataloguing-in-Publication Data
A catalogue record for this book is available from the British Library

ISBN 0 600 5954 39

Printed in China

Notes:
Both metric and imperial measures have been given in all recipes. Use one
set of measurements only and not a mixture of both.

Standard level spoon measurements are used in all recipes:
1 tablespoon = one 15 ml spoon
1 teaspoon = one 5 ml spoon

Eggs should be medium (sizes 2 and 3) unless otherwise stated.

Milk should be full fat unless otherwise stated.

Pepper should be freshly ground unless otherwise stated.

Fresh herbs should be used unless otherwise stated. If unavailable use
dried herbs as an alternative but halve the given quantities.

Ovens should be preheated to the specified temperature – if using a fan
assisted oven, follow the manufacturer's instructions for adjusting the time
and temperature.

traditional flavours from northern africa

Hilaire Walden

photography by David Loftus

contents

introduction

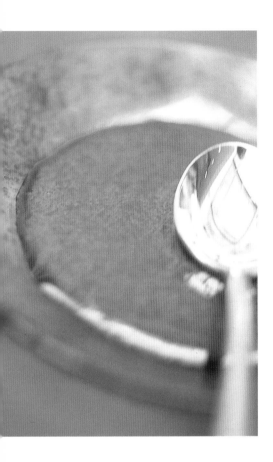

Moroccan food is one of the most sensual in the world. It appeals directly and unashamedly to the senses of smell, sight and taste in a way that no other cuisine can match. It is not only the cooked dishes that have this power to entice; many of the ingredients weave their own individual magic. The souks are magical places, with smells, sights and sounds that make one feel hungry just thinking of them. The glinting silveriness of very fresh fish, the mounds of vegetables with their different glowing colours, and the gradations of the muted hues of spices. Around every corner, waft different smells to surprise and delight – the fragrance of fresh bread as it bakes, the luxurious aroma of saffron, the sweet haunting smell of rosewater, then a light breeze rings the contrasting note of fresh mint. A few paces on, around another bend, and you are greeted by the unmistakable savoury smell of meat being seared over a charcoal brazier. Indeed, it is these very aromas that are the essence and defining points of Moroccan cooking.

The same character will be noticed in the neighbouring countries of Algeria and Tunisia, but each has its own identifiable style. Whereas Moroccan food exudes rich flavours, Algerian dishes are less richly spiced while Tunisians prefer a more lavish use of chillies, making theirs the hottest cuisine of the region. There are, though, many similarities and shared themes throughout the three countries: slow-simmered tagines, charcoal-grilled lamb, chicken, fish and vegetables, and rich, sweet pastries.

The Moroccan cuisine, as well as the cuisines of the rest of north Africa, is made up of contrasts stemming from the contrasting countryside (largely barren desert but with lush plains near the sea and the coast) and lifestyles of the nomadic tribes and the city dwellers. So, there are heavy, slowly cooked casseroles, simple small morsels of food quickly cooked over a white-hot charcoal fire, and sophisticated pies and other creations that require brigades of skilled chefs. All these elements sit happily side-by-side to make extremely exciting eating.

Moroccan hospitality is legendary. It is a part of the routine of life to provide what seems to us like an over-abundance; not only will there be a number of dishes but they will be piled high. Food will be provided to feed family, friends and any casual guest who happens to call in or pass by, as well as the women, children and servants who inhabit the kitchen. Moroccans also have hearty appetites and tend to eat until they are fully satisfied, the state they call *shaban*; no Moroccan worth his salt would ever leave the table feeling as if he could eat the same again, as we are told is polite to do.

Eating is serious business. In the middle and upper class Moroccan homes meals are eaten in dignified surroundings and served with formal elegance, although the actual eating of the food may appear to Western eyes to be less genteel. Typically, dining room walls are decorated with mosaics, and richly woven carpets cover the floors. Hand-carved low divans swamped by luxurious, elaborately decorated cushions line the sides of the room and a heavy circular table is laid with ornate baroque silverware and copperware, but there is no cutlery on the table because it is eschewed for eating. Chunks of bread are used for scooping up morsels of food from the communal dish and carrying it to the mouth, and for mopping up sauces. The thumb, forefinger and middle finger of the right hand are used (the left is considered unclean); to eat with one finger is considered a sign of hatred, to eat with two shows pride, while three accords with the Prophet Mohammed, whereas to eat with four or five fingers is a sign of gluttony.

Before the meal begins the hand-washing ceremony is performed. The host snaps his fingers and a servant circulates with a bowl of perfumed water, holding it beneath each person's hands, pouring water over them from an ornate copper kettle into an intricately decorated copper basin. A towel is offered for drying the hands. A number of dishes are placed on the table and everyone helps themselves directly from these dishes.

ingredients

Couscous

This is an extremely versatile ingredient that can be used in similar ways to rice but, to me, is far more interesting. Couscous is made from semolina that has been ground, moistened and rolled in flour. The preparation of couscous used to be a lengthy business but the couscous on sale nowadays is precooked and needs only to be moistened and steamed to heat it through and separate the grains. Butter, or *smen*, is often rubbed into the couscous to help the grains to separate and enrich them.

Well-prepared couscous should be soft and fluffy. To achieve this, put the couscous into a bowl, sprinkle over the required amount of water (the greater the ratio of water, the softer and less nutty the grain will be) and leave for 10–15 minutes, or until the water has been absorbed. Using your fingers, gently separate the grains, which should take 2–3 minutes, rubbing in some butter or oil if you like). Pile the grains into a fine meshed sieve or a colander lined with muslin or cheesecloth and put it over a saucepan of boiling water; making sure the bottom of the sieve or colander is well above the level of the water. Lightly cover the top of the couscous with a piece of muslin or a J-cloth, if you like. Steam until the couscous is hot throughout and there are small holes between the grains. Depending on the quantity of couscous this will take 15–30 minutes. Halfway through cooking, bring the lower half of the couscous to the top, so it is heated evenly, and rub in or fork through more butter or oil, if you like. To serve, mound the hot couscous on a warmed serving dish. Couscous is eaten by forming the grains into marble-sized balls between the fingers, a technique that requires practice.

Flower waters

The heady scents of both rosewater and orange flower water perfume not only many of the sticky sweet pastries and puddings, but are added to savoury dishes giving them a haunting flavour; B'stilla (see page 99) is the most well-known example; in Tunisia orange flower water is amongst the ingredients of meatballs. In Morocco flower waters are also used to perfume the water used for washing the hands before or after eating. Many homes make their own flower waters by the ancient method of distillation using an alembic still.

Herbs

Three herbs, coriander, flat leaf parsley and mint, are used very freely in Moroccan cooking and are part of the national flavour. But, apart from these, herbs do not feature very prominently in Moroccan or north African cooking.

Olive oil

Most Moroccan cooks use olive oil with a very generous hand. The oil serves not only to moisten ingredients that are fried and prevent them burning but also to flavour the dish, bind together the ingredients, and thicken dishes such as tagines. I have reduced the amounts of oil in my recipes to suit Western palates.

Olives

Many different varieties of olives grow in Morocco and north Africa; if you visit any good souk you will find stalls devoted entirely to displays of olives of varying sizes, meatiness, colours and hues. Each type will have its own special flavour, which in turn will give a characteristic flavour to the dish in which it is used.

Green olives are unripe olives while black ones are the fully ripe fruit. In general, three types of olives are used in Moroccan cooking: cracked green or whole green olives are added to salads and chicken dishes featuring lemon; almost ripe olives whose colour

has darkened to anywhere from a greenish tan to violet or wine red appear in more richly flavoured chicken tagines and with sharp lamb and fish recipes.

We are unable to buy anywhere near the variety of olives available in the *Magreb* but there is now a far greater selection available, so do try to find a variety that is as near as possible to the type specified in the recipe. It is possible to substitute any type of olive for another, but the result will be a very different-tasting dish, especially if you use a completely different colour of olive.

Ouarka

Pronounced *warka*, this is the wafer-thin pastry that is used for *b'stilla* (see page 99) and *briks* (see page 21). To make *ouarka* is a very skilled task and few people nowadays have the patience and skill involved. Making *ouarka* involves patting small balls of dough 18 or 20 times in succession in a series of concentric circles, overlapping the circles slightly, on a domed metal surface that is heated over a *canoon* to make a wide, circular sheet of delicate extremely thin, lacy pastry. Most people prefer to buy their pastry ready-made from specialist shops. Filo pastry is the substitute for Western cooks or, in some recipes, Chinese spring roll wrappers may be used.

Smen

This is the Moroccan version of Indian *ghee*, preserved clarified butter, although in the case of *smen* it may be flavoured with wild herbs. The distinctive cheesy flavour of *smen* gets stronger with age and takes some getting used to; the colour also darkens as the smen matures. *Smen* adds a characteristic taste to dishes such as Red-cooked Moroccan Chicken (see page 88), tagines and couscous.

If you would like your cooking to be as authentic as possible, a simplified method of making *smen* is easy. Gently heat 500 g (1 lb) diced unsalted butter until it has melted then increase the heat and bring the butter to the boil. Simmer for 3–4 minutes then remove from the heat; the butter will settle above a milky sediment. Wring out a piece of muslin or cheesecloth in hot water and use to line a sieve. Sprinkle about ¼ teaspoon dried *herbes de Provence* over the muslin or cheesecloth. Using a large metal spoon, carefully spoon the clarified butter into the sieve, allowing each spoonful to almost drain through before adding the next. Strain the butter for a second time, this time into a clean, dry jar. Cover and keep in the refrigerator for up to six weeks.

Spices

Cumin, coriander, ginger, paprika, nutmeg, cinnamon, allspice, cloves, saffron and turmeric are the most frequently used spices and will appear time and time again. They are used in different combinations of varying proportions to produce endlessly fascinating gradations of flavours and effects.

Use pure saffron threads in preference to the powder which may have been adulterated. A mere pinch of saffron is all that is needed to flavour a dish for 4–6 people, so threads are not as expensive as they may first seem. Gently and lightly roasting the saffron threads in a dry, heavy frying pan will bring out the flavour, and crushing them before adding to a dish will help them to dissolve more quickly.

Ras el hanout literally means 'top of the shop'. It is an old, complicated mixture of at least ten, often as many as 20 or 25 powdered spices, roots, barks and flowers. Every shopkeeper has his own special blend, which is kept a secret.

Bread

Bread is considered Allah's most precious gift and must be treated with respect; according to a local story, a woman who defiled a loaf was imprisoned in the moon. If bread is seen lying on the ground it must be picked up, kissed, a blessing invoked on it and then put somewhere to keep clean. At dinner, it is customary for the host to follow the age-old ritual of breaking a loaf apart and offering a piece to each guest.

moroccan kitchens

Moroccan kitchens are austere and very sparsely equipped, even in modern urban homes. Labour is cheap and plentiful so tasks are done by hand, by women, not by equipment or gadgets. Weighing equipment is rare because measuring is done by eye and feel. There is also a lack of ovens, even in restaurant kitchens; food that requires baking is taken to the communal bakehouse.

Chairs are seldom seen in traditional kitchens and even a table may well be absent; cooks squat both when mixing and cooking. There may be a stool or two, or perhaps an old carpet folded to form a seat for the cook.

A typical kitchen may contain an assortment of tagines (*touagen slaoui*), a deep copper dish (*ga tagine*) for holding the *tagine slaoui* during serving to protect the table from the hot pot, and a round shallow, woven straw basket (*tbeq*) for rolling couscous grain. A large ceramic platter (*kesria*) holds the grain.

There will be a brass mortar and pestle (*mehraz*), essential for grinding herbs and spice mixtures, a wooden ladle (*mghorfa*), carved from a single piece of orange or olive wood and a bulbous *rashasha* with a long stem-like spout which is used for sprinkling orange flower water and rosewater. A glazed earthenware pot (*genura*), which is very wide in relation to its height, is used for storing water, while fairly high but not very wide earthenware jars, which are glazed on the inside, hold preserved meats, flour, corn and pulses.

For cooking on, there will be the small round charcoal brazier (*canoon*), which lies at the heart of Moroccan cooking. It is specially designed to hold the round bottom of a tagine safely in place with its three raised points. The low, even heat that can be achieved with a charcoal fire is ideal for the slow-cooking that tagines need if they are to be at their most succulent and flavoursome. On the other hand, charcoal can be made sufficiently hot to produce the fierce heat that is required for succulent, tasty kebabs and other grilled foods. Metal *ghazels* are used for grilling kebabs and a hinged *chouaya* or *chebqua* for cooking fish over the *canoon*.

Another vital piece of equipment is the *gsaa*, the large wooden platter that is used daily in the preparation of bread dough. Spellings of the dishes and cooking equipment vary from place to place.

Tagine slaoui

This is a shallow, round earthenware glazed pot with a tall, conical lid like a Chinese coolie's hat, that traps the steam rising from the stew cooked in the bottom and prevents the stew drying out during the lengthy cooking time. Tagines come in all sizes; the smallest are suitable for an individual serving and are often seen in restaurants, while larger ones can be anything up to 60 cm (24 inches) across. Whatever the size of the tagine there is always a *canoon* that fits it snugly. Although many tagines have a clear glaze over the brown earthenware, some are richly decorated with intricate patterns in strong colours. If you are using a traditional north African tagine on a gas, electric or solid fuel hob it is best to use a heat-diffusing mat to protect the pot (but check with the cooker manufacturers' handbook for special electric hobs such as halogen). A heavy cast-iron tagine is now available from good kitchen shops. It is also perfectly acceptable to use a casserole dish with a tightly fitting lid, that you already have at home, as a substitute for the *tagine slaoui*.

Couscousier

The traditional pot for cooking couscous, this may be made from unglazed earthenware, tin-lined copper or aluminium, and comes in two parts – a lower pot in which the meat or vegetable stew part of the recipe is cooked, and an upper section with a perforated base to hold the grain. The aromatic steam from the stew permeates through the holes and heats the grain. A large sieve or a colander lined with muslin or cheesecloth may be used instead of a couscousier.

soups, starters & snacks

Moroccan soups are usually hearty and spicy and provide a sustaining supper. The best-known Moroccan soup is Harira (see page 14), which is drunk at sunset to break the day-long fasts during the holy month of Ramadan. At the start of a Moroccan meal a selection of dishes may be served together; then they are often left on the table for the rest of the meal. A number of these dishes are called 'salads' but they differ from Western salads by being purées, and are eaten as dips; for example Roast Squash Salad (see page 29). Most of the dishes in this chapter can be served as snacks, either on their own or as part of a selection.

fish soup

3 tablespoons olive oil

2 onions, chopped

2 celery sticks, sliced

4 garlic cloves, crushed

1 fresh red chilli, deseeded
and chopped

½ teaspoon ground cumin

1 cinnamon stick

½ teaspoon ground coriander

2 large potatoes, chopped

1.5 litres (2½ pints) fish and
shellfish stock, or water

3 tablespoons lemon juice

2 kg (4 lb) mixed fish and
shellfish, prepared

4 well-flavoured tomatoes, skinned,
deseeded if liked, and chopped

1 large bunch mixed dill,
parsley and coriander, chopped

salt and pepper

As in most places where men make their living from the sea, along the Moroccan and North African coasts as much of the catch as possible is used. What is not suitable for simple cooking is turned into fish soups. Any selection of fish and shellfish can be used for fish soup, with the exception of oily fish like mackerel and sardines. The trimmings, heads, tails, bones and shells can be used to make the fish stock.

1 Heat the oil in a large saucepan. Add the onion and celery and fry gently until softened and transparent, adding the garlic and chilli towards the end. Add the cumin, cinnamon and coriander and stir for 1 minute, then add the potatoes and cook, stirring, for a further 2 minutes.

2 Add the stock or water and the lemon juice. Heat to simmering point then simmer gently, uncovered, for about 20 minutes until the potatoes are tender.

3 Add the fish and shellfish, the tomatoes, herbs and salt and pepper and cook gently until the fish and shellfish are tender.

Serves 6–8

harira

2 tablespoons olive oil

250 g (8 oz) lean lamb, cubed

1 onion, chopped

125 g (4 oz) chickpeas, soaked
overnight and drained

1.5 litres (2½ pints) water

125 g (4 oz) red lentils

425 g (14 oz) tomatoes, skinned,
deseeded and chopped

1 tablespoon sun-dried tomato
paste

1 teaspoon ground cinnamon

1 red pepper, cored, deseeded
and chopped

50 g (2 oz) long-grain rice

1 bunch of coriander, chopped

salt and pepper

*As the sun sets on each hungry day during the fast month of Ramadan, a cannon fires
signalling that at last it is time to break the fast and eat a bowl of steaming, rich, colourful
and spicy harira.*

1 Heat the oil in a large saucepan, add the lamb and fry, stirring, until the pieces are
an even light brown. Stir in the onion and cook gently until softened.

2 Add the chickpeas and water and bring to the boil. Lower the heat, cover the pan
and simmer for 1 hour, until the chickpeas are tender.

3 Add the lentils, tomatoes, tomato paste, cinnamon and red pepper and simmer for
about 15 minutes.

4 Add the rice and simmer for a further 15 minutes, until the rice and lentils are tender.
Stir in the coriander, season to taste with salt and pepper and serve.

Serves 6

lamb soup with chickpeas & couscous

2 tablespoons olive oil

175 g (6 oz) lean lamb, finely chopped

1 large onion, chopped

3 garlic cloves, crushed

1 fresh red chilli, deseeded and finely chopped

1½ teaspoons cumin seeds, roasted and crushed

1½ teaspoons coriander seeds, roasted and crushed

1½ teaspoons ground allspice

875 g (28 oz) can chopped tomatoes

2 tablespoons tomato purée

900 ml (1½ pints) veal or vegetable stock

125 g (4 oz) chickpeas, soaked overnight and drained

2 tablespoons chopped parsley

1 tablespoon chopped mint

50 g (2 oz) couscous

about 2 teaspoons sugar

salt and pepper

lemon wedges, to serve

To roast and crush the cumin and coriander seeds, heat a small, heavy frying pan, add the spice seeds and dry-fry until they smell fragrant. Tip them into a spice grinder and pulverize or put them into a mortar and crush with a pestle. Alternatively, put them into a bowl and crush them with the end of a rolling pin.

1 Heat the oil in a large heavy-based saucepan. Add the lamb to the pan and brown quickly. Using a slotted spoon, transfer the lamb to kitchen paper to drain. Stir the onion into the pan and cook until soft and browned, adding the garlic and chilli when the onion is almost cooked.

2 Add the cumin and coriander seeds and allspice and stir for 1 minute.

3 Return the lamb to the pan and add the tomatoes, tomato purée, stock and chickpeas. Stir well then cover the pan and simmer very gently for about 1 hour until the chickpeas are tender.

4 Stir the parsley, mint and couscous into the soup, cover and remove from the heat. Add the sugar and salt and pepper to taste. Serve accompanied by lemon wedges.

Serves 6

chickpea soup

Instead of serving this recipe as a chunky soup, it can be puréed and served with a little extra virgin olive oil swirled into each serving.

1 Heat the oil in a saucepan. Add the onion and garlic and fry for 5–7 minutes until softened and beginning to brown. Add the paprika, coriander and cumin and stir for 2 minutes.

2 Add the thyme, chilli flakes, chickpeas and stock. Bring to the boil then cover the pan and simmer the soup for 40 minutes.

3 Add the potato, carrots, celery, tomatoes and coriander to the pan. Cover and simmer for a further 30–40 minutes until the chickpeas and vegetables are tender.

4 Season to taste and serve with more coriander scattered over the top.

Serves 4–6

4 tablespoons olive oil

1 onion, chopped

3 garlic cloves, crushed

1 tablespoon paprika

1 tablespoon ground coriander

2 teaspoons ground cumin

2 thyme sprigs

pinch of dried chilli flakes

250 g (8 oz) chickpeas, soaked overnight and drained

1.5 litres (2½ pints) vegetable stock

1 large potato, chopped

2 carrots, sliced

2 celery sticks, sliced

3 tomatoes, chopped

3 tablespoons chopped fresh coriander

salt and pepper

chopped fresh coriander, to garnish

split pea soup

1 Put the split peas, onion, half of the garlic, the mint sprigs and olive oil into a large saucepan. Add enough water to cover generously and bring to the boil. Lower the heat, cover the pan and simmer for about 35 minutes or until the split peas are very tender. Remove the lid towards the end of the cooking, if necessary; the split peas should be just covered with water.

2 Meanwhile, put the remaining garlic, spring onions, ground coriander, chilli flakes, coriander leaves, mint and butter into a bowl and crush to a paste. Cover and store in the refrigerator until required.

3 Transfer two-thirds of the split peas and their liquid to a food processor or blender, purée until smooth then return to the pan. Simmer for a few minutes until thickened to the required consistency, then season to taste with salt and pepper. Serve the soup in warmed bowls with a knob of the spiced butter floating on top.

Serves 6

425 g (15 oz) yellow or
green split peas

1 large onion, chopped

4 garlic cloves, crushed

3 large mint sprigs

3 tablespoons extra virgin olive oil

2 spring onions, finely chopped

1 teaspoon ground coriander

small pinch of dried chilli flakes

small handful of coriander
leaves, chopped

2 tablespoons chopped mint

50 g (2 oz) unsalted butter

salt and pepper

spiced chickpeas

400 g (13 oz) can chickpeas,
drained and rinsed

2 tablespoons olive oil

2 plump garlic cloves, crushed

paprika and ground cumin,
for sprinkling

salt and pepper

Snacking is a comparatively recent eating trend in Britain; in Morocco they have been doing it for generations and are past-masters at producing a myriad of moreish nibbles throughout the day. Deep-fried spiced dried broad beans are a particular speciality, but because it is much easier for us to get chickpeas I am giving a recipe using them. Baking is more in line with modern eating and cooking, so I have modified the traditional method.

1 Spread the chickpeas on a baking sheet. Mix the oil with the garlic and pour over the chickpeas, stirring everything together.

2 Transfer the baking sheet to a preheated oven, 200°C (400°F), Gas Mark 6, and cook the chickpeas for about 15 minutes, stirring them occasionally so they cook evenly.

3 Tip the chickpeas on to kitchen paper to dry them, then toss while still warm with paprika, cumin and salt and pepper. Eat while warm or store in an airtight jar in a cool place for up to 2 weeks.

Serves 2–4

aubergine & cheese sandwiches

1 aubergine, weighing 375 g (12 oz), cut into 5 mm (¼ inch) round slices

125 g (4 oz) ricotta or cream cheese

15 g (½ oz) Parmesan cheese, freshly grated

½ garlic clove, crushed

2 eggs, beaten (separately)

1½ tablespoons chopped mixed herbs, such as parsley, mint, dill and chives, plus more for the garnish

olive oil, for brushing and frying

50 g (2 oz) toasted breadcrumbs

salt and pepper

The smell of a batch of these cooking drew me to a stall in Marrakesh's medina, where a boy, about 16 years old, was forming the 'sandwiches', tossing them into the blackened pan of hot oil and always retrieving the right ones at the right moment, with all the aplomb of a seasoned expert.

1 Put the aubergine slices into a colander, sprinkle them with salt and leave them to drain for 30–60 minutes. Rinse the slices and dry well.

2 Mash the ricotta, Parmesan and garlic with one of the beaten eggs, then stir in the mixed herbs and season with salt and pepper.

3 Brush the aubergine slices with oil, place under a preheated grill and cook until browned on both sides. Drain on kitchen paper.

4 Cut each aubergine slice in half. Spread the cheese mixture on half of them, then cover neatly with the remaining halves and press lightly together.

5 Put the toasted breadcrumbs into a shallow dish and the remaining beaten egg into a bowl. Dip the aubergine 'sandwiches' into the egg, allow the excess to drain away, then coat evenly with the breadcrumbs.

6 Heat the oil until hot, add the 'sandwiches' and fry them for 1½ minutes on each side until golden and crisp. Drain the 'sandwiches' on kitchen paper and serve hot, garnished with finely chopped herbs.

Serves 4

briks

Briks *(pronounced* breeks*) are* ouarka *turnovers that originate in Tunisia. The Pieds Noirs, or Blackfeet (Europeans born in the Magreb) were responsible for spreading their popularity throughout North Africa. Traditionally* briks *are deep-fried and have to be served immediately they are cooked otherwise they become heavy and greasy, but they can be baked.*

1 To make the filling, finely chop the olives and anchovy fillets together then mix them with the tomatoes, almonds, mixed coriander and parsley, eggs and lemon juice and season with pepper.

2 Cut the pastry into 10 x 25 cm (4 x 10 inch) strips. Work with 3 or 4 strips at a time; keeping the remaining pastry covered with clingfilm.

3 Brush the strips lightly with oil and put a heaped teaspoon of the filling at the top right-hand corner of each one. Fold the corner down to make a triangle. Continue folding the triangle along the length of the strip. Place on a baking sheet and brush with oil. Repeat until all the filling has been used.

4 Sprinkle the briks with sesame seeds and bake in a preheated oven, 190°C (375°F), Gas Mark 5, for about 20 minutes until crisp and golden. Serve hot or warm.

Makes about 24

about 250 g (8 oz) filo pastry, thawed if frozen

olive oil, for brushing

sesame seeds, for sprinkling

Filling:

50 g (2 oz) olives, pitted

3 anchovy fillets

3 sun-dried tomatoes in oil, drained and chopped

2 tablespoons chopped almonds

2 tablespoons chopped mixed coriander and parsley

3 soft-boiled eggs, chopped

squeeze of lemon juice, to taste

pepper

merguez pastries

These are a version of briouts *(pronounced* breewats*), Moroccan cigar or triangular-shaped* ouarka *pastries. The fillings for* briouts *are many and varied, ranging from minced brains to rice pudding! More usual are the minced lamb mixture used for keftas, the filling for* b'stilla, *tuna and eggs. Normally deep-fried (because of the absence of convenient ovens) they can also be baked. Uncooked* briouts *freeze well.*

250 g (8 oz) fresh spinach, washed but not dried

75 g (3 oz) Merguez sausage (see page 25), cut into 5 mm (¼ inch) dice

75 g (3 oz) low-fat soft cheese

about 150 g (5 oz) filo pastry

olive oil, for brushing

salt and pepper

1 Put the spinach into a large saucepan, cover and cook until the leaves have wilted. Tip the spinach into a colander and squeeze out as much water as possible. Chop the spinach and leave to cool.

2 Put the sausage into a dry heavy frying pan and cook until browned. Transfer to kitchen paper to drain and cool.

3 Mix together the spinach, sausage and cheese. Season to taste with salt and pepper.

4 Cut the filo pastry into 7.5 cm (3 inch) squares and cover with clingfilm to prevent them drying out. Brush 1 square with oil and put another on top. Oil the second square then put a little of the merguez mixture in a short sausage shape near one edge. Fold in the adjoining sides then roll up the pastry to enclose the filling. Place the pastry, seam-side down, on a greased baking sheet. Brush the top with oil. Repeat with the remaining pastry and filling.

5 Bake the pastries in a preheated oven, 200°C (400°F), Gas Mark 6, for 10–12 minutes until golden. Serve warm.

Makes about 24

mussel & tomato pastries

The most unusual mussel dish that I've eaten in Morocco was based on sun-dried mussels; they were combined with olives and chillies as part of a massive first-course spread. These deep-fried pillows will have a wider appeal – crisp, thin sheets of pastry shatter as you bite through them into the yielding succulent mussel within. The juicy tomatoes complete the texture and taste sensations.

1 Bring about 2.5 cm (1 inch) salted water to the boil in a large saucepan. Add the mussels, cover the pan and allow the mussels to steam for 2–3 minutes, tossing the pan frequently, until the shells open. Tip the mussels into a colander and discard any that remain closed. Remove the mussels from their shells.

2 Heat the oil in a saucepan over a low heat, add the tomatoes and simmer until soft. Drain through a sieve, retaining the juices and reserving the tomatoes. Pour the juices back into the saucepan, add the garlic and lemon juice and boil until syrupy. Leave to cool, then add the tomatoes, mussels and parsley and season with salt and pepper.

3 Place the sheets of filo pastry on top of each other, brushing each one with oil. Cut into twelve 10 x 10 cm (4 x 4 inch) squares. Wet the edges. Spoon 2 mussels with some of the sauce on to each square, then fold the pastry over and press the edges together to seal.

4 Oil a baking sheet and place the pastries on it. Glaze the tops with melted butter or beaten egg and bake in a preheated oven, 200°C (400°F), Gas Mark 6, for 10–12 minutes until golden. Carefully transfer the pastries to a wire rack. Serve warm or at room temperature.

Makes 12

24 mussels, scrubbed and debearded

2 tablespoons olive oil, plus extra for brushing

3 tomatoes, skinned, deseeded and cut into 8 pieces each

1 small garlic clove, crushed

1½ tablespoons lemon juice

1½ tablespoons finely chopped parsley

about 2 sheets filo pastry

melted butter or beaten egg, for glazing

salt and pepper

keftas

In Morocco the meat for keftas is finely chopped by hand with a heavy steel knife, then pounded or kneaded with the flavourings until the mixture is almost as smooth as a paste. Traditional keftas usually contain about ten per cent fat; this binds the ingredients together and keeps the keftas moist during cooking. Less fatty keftas are preferred by most people today, especially in the West, but this does mean that the keftas will be more dry and crumbly. Freshly minced meat will give the best results.

1 Mix all the ingredients together with your hands, season with salt and pepper and knead to make a homogenous paste; this may take up to 15 minutes. Cover and chill for 15 minutes.

2 Form the mixture into sausage shapes about 2 cm (¾ inch) thick. Grill or barbecue on an oiled rack for about 5 minutes on each side until cooked to your liking.

3 Serve the keftas sprinkled with a mixture of salt and cumin.

Serves 4

625 g (1¼ lb) boneless lamb, freshly minced

1 onion, grated

2 garlic cloves, crushed

1 tablespoon paprika

1 teaspoon ground cumin

¼ teaspoon ground cinnamon

¼ teaspoon cayenne pepper

bunch of coriander, finely chopped

several mint leaves, chopped

1 egg, beaten

salt and pepper

salt and ground cumin, to serve

merguez

Merguez are the region's sausages. They are slim, reddened by paprika and fragrant from the use of North African aromatic spices. They should be well-flavoured; to test if the level and balance of seasoning is to your liking, before filling the skins, break off a small piece of the mixture and fry it until cooked through before tasting. Merguez can be eaten hot or cold.

1 Pass the beef, beef fat and garlic through a mincer into a bowl. Add the ground cinnamon, cloves, paprika, cayenne pepper and dried thyme and season with salt and pepper. Mix together thoroughly with your hands, adding enough water to moisten the mixture. Cover the bowl and leave in the refrigerator for a few hours.

2 Using a food mixer with a sausage attachment or a piping bag fitted with a large plain nozzle, carefully fill the sausage casings with the sausage mixture, tying or twisting at 2.5–5 cm (1–2 inch) intervals. Hang the sausages to dry in a dry, airy, warmish place for 24 hours.

3 Fry or grill the sausages, turning occasionally, until lightly browned.

Serves 4–6

375 g (12 oz) beef, cubed

125 g (4 oz) beef fat, cubed

1–2 garlic cloves, crushed

1 teaspoon ground cinnamon

1 teaspoon ground cloves

1 teaspoon ground paprika

1 teaspoon cayenne pepper

1 teaspoon crumbled dried thyme

2–4 tablespoons chilled water

sausage casings

salt and pepper

quick mixed pickled vegetables

Serve with drinks or as part of an hors d'oeurve.

1 Sprinkle the vegetables with salt and leave for 2–4 hours then rinse the vegetables thoroughly and dry well.

2 Mix together the peppercorns, sugar and vinegar or lemon juice until the sugar has dissolved. Season with black pepper. Stir the dressing into the vegetables then cover and refrigerate overnight. Stir in the coriander and serve chilled.

Serves 4–6

125 g (4 oz) baby carrots

125 g (4 oz) small radishes

4 celery sticks, cut into 4 cm (1½ inch) lengths

1 cucumber, halved, deseeded and thickly sliced

1 tablespoon pink peppercorns

4 tablespoons caster sugar

4 tablespoons white wine vinegar or lemon juice

1 bunch of coriander, chopped

salt and pepper

eggs baked on red vegetables

5 tablespoons olive oil

1 Spanish onion, sliced

4 garlic cloves, crushed

4 red peppers, cored, deseeded and sliced

1 courgette, sliced

5 ripe, well-flavoured tomatoes, sliced

2 tablespoons chopped parsley

large pinch of paprika

large pinch of dried chilli flakes

4 eggs

salt and pepper

To garnish:

ground cumin

paprika

4 coriander sprigs

A rich, paprika-red garlicky mixture of slowly-cooked red peppers, tomatoes, onion and courgettes makes a bed full of flavour on which to cook eggs. The eggs should only be lightly cooked so that the yolks will flow as a contrasting creamy sauce over the vegetables.

1 Heat the oil in a large frying pan. Add the onion and fry briskly until golden. Add the garlic, red peppers, courgette and tomatoes and simmer for 15–20 minutes, stirring occasionally, until all the vegetables are soft.

2 Stir in the parsley, paprika and chilli flakes and season to taste with salt and pepper. Simmer for a further 5 minutes.

3 Spoon the vegetable mixture into a large shallow ovenproof dish. Make 4 indentations in the vegetable mixture and break an egg into each one. Bake in a preheated oven, 160°C (325°F), Gas Mark 3, for 10 minutes until the egg whites are just set and the yolks are still creamy.

4 To serve, sprinkle fine trails of ground cumin and paprika over·the eggs and garnish with sprigs of coriander.

Serves 4

dried broad bean dip

250 g (8 oz) dried broad beans, soaked overnight and drained

3 garlic cloves, crushed

1 teaspoon cumin seeds

virgin olive oil

salt

To serve:

za'atar (wild thyme) or mixed dried thyme, marjoram and oregano

bread

small bowl of mixed ground cumin, cayenne pepper and salt

Bessara, to give this dip its local name, is to North Africa what hummus is to the Middle East. The taste is also similar. Serve bessara with warm bread.

1 Put the dried broad beans, garlic and cumin into a saucepan. Add cold water to just cover and bring to the boil. Cover the pan and simmer for 1–2 hours, depending on the age and quality of the beans, until tender.

2 Drain the bean mixture, reserving the liquid, and purée in a food processor or blender, adding enough of the reserved bean liquid and oil to make a cream. Alternatively, rub through a sieve. Season with salt.

3 Serve the dip warm with extra oil trickled over the top and sprinkled with *za'atar* or mixed dried thyme, marjoram and oregano. Accompany with warm bread and a small bowl of mixed ground cumin, cayenne pepper and salt.

Serves 4–6

broad bean & mint dip

This very simple, fresh-tasting dip will undoubtedly be at its best if you use fresh young broad beans, but frozen ones will be quite acceptable. Serve with crudités or bread.

500 g (1 lb) shelled fresh broad beans

leaves from 6–8 mint sprigs

3–4 tablespoons olive oil

about 2 tablespoons lemon juice

salt and pepper

small mint sprigs, to garnish

1 Cook the broad beans in boiling salted water until tender. Drain, reserving the cooking liquid. Rinse the beans under running cold water.

2 Put the beans into a food processor or blender. Add the mint, olive oil and lemon juice and mix to a purée, adding enough of the reserved cooking liquid to give a soft consistency. Season to taste with salt and pepper and adjust the levels of lemon juice and oil, if necessary.

3 Transfer the dip to a small serving dish. Serve at room temperature, garnished with small mint sprigs.

Serves 4

roast squash salad

1 kg (2 lb) squash, cut into 8

6 garlic cloves, unpeeled

2 tablespoons extra virgin olive oil

1 tablespoon chopped thyme

2 hard-boiled eggs, quartered

salt and pepper

coriander leaves, to garnish

Dressing:

2 garlic cloves

5 tablespoons extra virgin olive oil

2 tablespoons red wine vinegar

1½ teaspoons caraway seeds

4 teaspoons Harissa (see page 80)

This is a puréed salad. The squash is roasted with garlic and thyme to bring out its flavour and drive off water, before being puréed with a spicy dressing. The result is a salad that is vibrant in taste and appearance. Ideally use butternut squash: they have the best flavour and texture and are now quite widely available for much of the year.

1 Put the squash and garlic into a shallow baking dish. Pour over the oil and sprinkle with the thyme and season with salt and pepper. Stir together then bake in a preheated oven, 180°C (350°F), Gas Mark 4, for about 1 hour until the squash is tender and slightly charred. Leave the squash and cooking juices to cool.

2 To make the dressing, mash the garlic with a pinch of salt then work in the oil drop by drop as if making mayonnaise. Stir in the vinegar, caraway seeds and harissa.

3 Peel and mash the roasted garlic. Remove the skin from the squash and discard. Chop the flesh then purée or mash it with the garlic and cooking juices.

4 Stir the dressing into the squash. Arrange the eggs on top and garnish with coriander leaves.

Serves 4–6

aubergine purée

Roasting then puréeing aubergines is possibly the best way of eating them because it highlights their wonderful seductive slippery quality. Once I've started I find it hard to resist scooping up this delectable purée for ages. A drawback can be the aubergine's tendancy to soak up oil like a sponge; I've kept the amount modest in this recipe but others are not as circumspect. Fortunately, aubergines have an affinity with olive oil, but it must be a good one.

2 aubergines, total weight about 625 g (1¼ lb)

2 garlic cloves, sliced

½ teaspoon ground cumin

1 teaspoon paprika

about 50 ml (2 fl oz) extra virgin olive oil, plus extra to serve

juice of 1 lemon

salt and pepper

mint or coriander, to garnish

1 Cut slits in the aubergines and insert the garlic slices. Bake in a preheated oven, 220°C (425°F), Gas Mark 7, for 30–40 minutes until the skins are charred and blistered. Remove from the oven and leave to cool.

2 Slice the aubergines in half and scoop out the flesh and the garlic slices. Squeeze out and discard the juices. Put the aubergine, garlic, cumin and paprika into a food processor and mix to a purée. With the motor running, slowly pour in the olive oil to give the consistency of a soft dip. Add lemon juice and salt and pepper to taste.

3 Transfer the purée to a bowl. With the back of a spoon, mark a spiral in the top. Just before serving, dribble over some olive oil and garnish with mint or coriander.

Serves 4

marinated courgettes

750 g (1½ lb) courgettes, cut into 5 mm (¼ inch) slices

olive oil

leaves from 1 bunch of basil

3 tablespoons mint leaves

2 small garlic cloves, finely chopped

2 tablespoons lemon juice

salt and pepper

Marinating is a very old method of food preservation. Nowadays, it is used simply as one of many ways of preparing foods, usually fish and vegetables. Here, the combination of courgettes, lemon and herbs makes a light and refreshing dish.

1 Layer the courgette slices with salt in a colander and leave to drain for 30 minutes. Rinse the courgettes well and pat dry.

2 Heat a 5 mm (¼ inch) layer of olive oil in a large frying pan, add the courgette slices in batches so they are not crowded and cook for about 3 minutes on each side until golden. Using a slotted spoon, transfer them to kitchen paper to drain.

3 Arrange the courgettes on a dish, tucking the basil and mint leaves among them and sprinkle with the garlic, lemon juice and salt and pepper. Cover and leave for at least 2 hours, preferably overnight, in the refrigerator, but return to room temperature about 30 minutes before serving.

Serves 4

marinated olives

500 g (1 lb) green or black olives

1 fresh red chilli, deseeded and chopped

4 garlic cloves, crushed

1 oregano sprig

1 thyme sprig

1 teaspoon finely chopped rosemary

2 bay leaves

1 teaspoon fennel seeds, bruised

1 teaspoon cumin seeds, roasted and finely crushed

olive oil

Gnarled, ancient, grey-green trees, their branches twisted in intricate patterns, are the cornerstone of the food of North Africa. Marinating olives with herbs and spices gives them additional distinction and is a way for a bar to personalize the olives it serves. If they are stored in a cool, dark place, these marinated olives will keep for several months.

1 Using a small sharp knife make a lengthways slit through to the stone of each olive. Put the olives into a bowl and stir in the chilli, garlic, oregano, thyme, rosemary, bay leaves, fennel seeds and cumin.

2 Pack the olive mixture into a screw-top jar and cover with olive oil. Close the jar and leave the olives for at least 3 days before using, shaking the jar occasionally.

Serves 4

pickled turnips

50 g (2 oz) coarse salt

500 ml (17 fl oz) water

250 ml (8 fl oz) white wine vinegar

1 kg (2 lb) small turnips, halved

1 small uncooked beetroot, peeled and sliced

2–4 garlic cloves (optional)

a few celery leaves

The small, sweet turnips from the lush coastal stretches of Morocco are ideal for pickling. These pretty pink vegetables have a delicate, sweet sharpness and light crispness that I found most appealing. The pickled turnips will keep for 2–3 months in the refrigerator.

1 Bring the salt and water to the boil over a low heat, stirring. Remove from the heat, add the vinegar and leave to cool.

2 Layer the turnips, beetroot slices, garlic, if using, and the celery leaves in a sterilized preserving jar. Pour the cooled brine over the vegetables to cover them completely. Slip a fine knife or skewer down the inside of the jar in several places to dislodge any air bubbles. Place a small saucer, or something similar that will fit inside the jar, over the turnips, with a weight on top if necessary. Close the jar tightly and leave on a sunny window sill, or any other warm place, for about 2 weeks.

Serves 4

prawn kebabs

1 Put the prawns into a glass or pottery bowl. Mix together the lemon juice, olive oil, garlic and mint, season with salt and pepper and pour over the prawns. Stir to coat the prawns with the dressing then leave for 30 minutes.

2 Thread the prawns on to skewers and cook under a preheated grill for about 3 minutes on each side until they turn pink.

3 Serve on a bed of salad, if you like, with lemon wedges.

Serves 4

20 raw tiger prawns, peeled and deveined, tails left intact

3 tablespoons lemon juice

1½ tablespoons virgin olive oil

2 garlic cloves, finely crushed

3 tablespoons chopped mint

salt and pepper

lemon wedges, to serve

lamb kebabs

Kebabs, piping hot, and charred and flavoured from cooking on a barbecue, are for me one of the most memorable and delightful aspects of Moroccan eating, indeed of Morocco. In England, such a pleasure is only possible on a few days during our short summer, and even then the kebabs don't taste quite the same.

1 Put the lamb into a bowl. Mix together all the marinade ingredients, add to the lamb and stir to mix thoroughly. Cover and leave at room temperature for 2 hours, or overnight in the refrigerator. If you put the lamb in the refrigerator, return it to room temperature 1 hour before cooking.

2 Remove the lamb from the marinade and pat dry. Thread the lamb on to 6 long skewers. Cook on a heated barbecue or under a preheated grill for 10–15 minutes, turning occasionally and brushing with any remaining marinade, until browned on the outside but still pink inside.

3 Serve on a bed of salad, if you like, with lemon wedges.

Serves 6

1 kg (2 lb) boned shoulder of lamb, cut into 5 cm (2 inch) cubes

lemon wedges, to serve

Marinade:

3 tablespoons olive oil

2 tablespoons lemon juice

1 garlic clove, crushed

1½ tablespoons paprika

1 teaspoon ground cumin

1 teaspoon ground coriander

1 teaspoon Harissa (see page 80)

seafood

Moroccan fish markets are a delight and fascination. They are also especially varied because the fishermen have access to the riches of the waters of the Mediterranean and the colder Atlantic, as well as the rivers and streams that flow down from the hills to the sea. Some of the diverse saltwater bounty might include mackerel, red mullet, sea bass, sardines, bream, anchovies, monkfish, sole, whiting, John Dory, skate, prawns, crab, lobsters, mussels and clams while freshwaters could yield a catch of pike or carp, bluefish, shad and trout.

trout stuffed with couscous, almonds & herbs

Couscous is often used as a stuffing for fish, meat and poultry. It makes a lighter, more open-textured filling than breadcrumbs, so I find that I am adapting more and more of my stuffing recipes to incorporate it. In this recipe, almonds provide an interesting textural contrast.

1 Heat 2 tablespoons of the oil in a frying pan, add the onion and fry until softened, adding the garlic towards the end. Stir in the couscous, fish or vegetable stock, parsley and mint. Bring to the boil then remove the pan from the heat and leave for 10–15 minutes until the liquid has been absorbed.

2 Season the trout with salt and pepper and fill the cavity of each one with a quarter of the couscous mixture. Lay the fish in a greased shallow baking dish. Mix the remaining oil with the almonds and spoon over the fish. Bake in a preheated oven, 200°C (400°F), Gas Mark 6, for 15–20 minutes until the fish flakes when tested with a fork.

3 Garnish with lemon wedges and mint sprigs and serve with warm bread.

Serves 4

4 tablespoons olive oil

1 small onion, finely chopped

2 garlic cloves, crushed

125 g (4 oz) couscous

300 ml (½ pint) fish or vegetable stock

1 tablespoon chopped parsley

1 tablespoon chopped mint

4 trout, each weighing about 375 g (12 oz), gutted, heads removed and boned

50 g (2 oz) flaked almonds

salt and pepper

To garnish:

lemon wedges

mint sprigs

tuna with spiced onion relish

When I dropped in on Fatima I had not realised that I was hungry, but the wonderful aromas of slowly cooking spices and onions that wafted from the kitchen literally made my mouth water. The dictates of Moroccan hospitality did not let me down so when the offer of lunch came I don't think I put up a very convincing display of the necessary preliminary reticence before accepting. The expectation was every bit as good as the reality.

1 Season the tuna sparingly with chilli powder. Cover and leave in a cool place for 1 hour.

2 Meanwhile, heat a dry heavy flameproof earthenware dish or heavy frying pan. Add the coriander, cumin, ginger, and season with salt and cayenne pepper, then dry-fry over a low heat for 30 seconds. Add the oil to the pan and heat for 30 seconds then add the onions and garlic. Cover and cook gently for about 45 minutes until the onions are golden and very soft.

3 Add the stock to the pan and put the fish on the onions, bring to simmering point then cook gently until the fish flakes when tested with a fork.

4 Transfer the fish to a warmed serving dish with a slotted spoon. Boil the mixture in the pan until most of the liquid has evaporated, then add to the fish on the dish and serve.

Serves 4

4 tuna steaks, each weighing about 175 g (6 oz)

chilli powder, to taste

1 tablespoon ground coriander

2 tablespoons ground cumin

2 tablepoons peeled and grated fresh root ginger

4 tablespoons olive oil

1 kg (2 lb) large onions, sliced

4 garlic cloves, crushed

100 ml (3½ fl oz) fish stock

salt and cayenne pepper

tuna with red pepper & olive sauce

In this recipe anchovy fillets add depth to the flavour of the sauce.

1 Season the tuna with pepper. Heat the oil in a large frying pan. Add the tuna and brown over a high heat for 2 minutes on each side. Remove with a slotted spoon to kitchen paper and keep warm. Add the garlic and red pepper to the pan and fry for 1–2 minutes until the garlic begins to colour. Stir in the anchovies so they start to dissolve then add the stock. Bring to the boil then simmer for 8–10 minutes.

2 Return the tuna to the pan and cook for about 4 minutes, basting frequently with the sauce, until cooked to your liking. Add the olives, lemon juice and parsley and serve immediately.

Serves 4

4 tuna steaks

3 tablespoons olive oil

1 garlic clove, crushed

1 red pepper, cored, deseeded and quite finely chopped

2 anchovy fillets, chopped

125 ml (4 fl oz) fish stock

125 g (4 oz) black olives, pitted and chopped

juice of ½ lemon, to taste

3 tablespoons chopped parsley

pepper

fish keftas

There is no denying that much of traditional Moroccan cooking can be rich, as I have found to my cost on more than one occasion; even though I try to avoid very oily dishes when in Morocco, if I want to experience genuine food of the country over a number of days I know that this will inevitably mean consuming more fat than normal. These keftas are a good antidote; though they are meaty, they are light. The keftas can be prepared ahead and kept covered in the refrigerator.

1 Mince the fish or chop it very finely by hand. Put it in a bowl and mix thoroughly with the fresh and ground coriander, mint, cumin, turmeric, butter and salt and pepper.

2 Shape the fish mixture into about 20 small oval shapes and thread on to skewers. Chill for about 30 minutes.

3 Cook the keftas under a preheated hot grill for 3–4 minutes, turning occasionally.

Serves 4

250 g (8 oz) cod, skinned

2 teaspoons chopped coriander

1 teaspoon ground coriander

2 teaspoons chopped mint

1 teaspoon ground cumin

½ teaspoon ground turmeric

2 tablespoons melted butter

salt and pepper

carp with raisins & almonds

1 Season the fish steaks and put them into an earthenware dish that they just fit.

2 Heat 1 tablespoon of the oil in a heavy frying pan, add the almonds and fry gently until lightly browned.

3 Add the remaining oil to the pan, then stir in the raisins and spice mixture. Heat for 1 minute then pour over the fish. Cover the dish securely and bake in a preheated oven, 200°C (400°F), Gas Mark 6, for 25–30 minutes until fish just flakes when tested with a fork.

4 Serve the steaks with the juices spooned over. Garnish with parsley sprigs and serve with orange wedges to squeeze over.

Serves 4

4 carp steaks, about 4 cm
(1½ inches) thick

2 tablespoons olive oil

50 g (2 oz) flaked almonds

50 g (2 oz) plump raisins

1¼ teaspoons mixed ground
cinnamon, cumin, allspice and
mace

salt and pepper

parsley sprigs, to garnish

orange wedges, to serve

monkfish with mint

Safi is a coastal town known for its seafood dishes. This particular recipe comes from a modern Safi cook who has tinged his mother's traditional family dish with a light touch.

1 Brush the monfkish with olive oil, then season with salt and rub with the cut sides of the chilli. Cover and set aside for 1 hour.

2 Cook the monkfish under a preheated grill for about 4 minutes on each side until the flesh just flakes when tested with a fork.

3 Meanwhile, put 6 tablespoons of the oil, the tomatoes, garlic, shallot, mint and parsley into a small saucepan and heat until the garlic begins to sizzle and the tomatoes soften.

4 Whisk together the lime juice, vinegar and the remaining 2 tablespoons of olive oil, then slowly pour in the warm olive oil, whisking all time. Season with salt and cayenne pepper. Spoon the dressing over the fish and serve.

Serves 4

4 monkfish fillets, each weighing
about 175 g (6 oz)

8 tablespoons extra virgin olive oil,
plus extra for brushing

1 fresh red chilli, halved
lengthways

4 tomatoes, deseeded and chopped

2 garlic cloves, crushed

1 shallot, finely chopped

3 tablespoons chopped mint

1 tablespoon chopped parsley

1 tablespoon lime juice

2 tablespoons red wine vinegar

salt and cayenne pepper

fish & fennel tagine

This dish is of Safi origin. Any firm white fish such as cod, haddock or monkfish can be used.

4 tablespoons virgin olive oil

1 onion, chopped

3 garlic cloves, crushed

½ fennel bulb, thinly sliced

¼–½ teaspoon fennel seeds

500 g (1 lb) ripe, well-flavoured tomatoes, chopped

1–2 teaspoons sun-dried tomato paste

4 cod or other fish steaks, each weighing about 175 g (6 oz)

½ bunch parsley, chopped

juice and grated rind of 1 lemon

salt and pepper

chopped parsley, to garnish

1 Heat 2 tablespoons of the oil in a frying pan, add the onion, garlic, fennel and fennel seeds and fry until the onion is softened. Stir in the tomatoes and continue to cook for about 2 minutes, then add the tomato paste and simmer gently, uncovered, for about 15 minutes, stirring occasionally. Season to taste with salt and pepper, then set aside.

2 Heat the remaining oil in a frying pan. Add the fish and brown quickly on both sides. Transfer to kitchen paper to drain. Wipe out the pan, if liked.

3 Off the heat, lay the parsley in the bottom of a heavy flameproof earthenware dish that the fish will just fit in a single layer. Put the fish on top and sprinkle with the lemon juice and rind. Pour over the sauce and heat to simmering point. Cook very gently, uncovered, for 10–15 minutes until the fish just flakes when tested with the point of a sharp knife. Serve garnished with chopped parsley.

Serves 4

fish tagine with chermoula

Whenever I see a dish cooked with or in chermoula I am always tempted to try it; every one is different and there seems no end to the sometimes subtle, sometimes striking differences that there can be between chermoula recipes.

750 g (1½ lb) grey mullet, bream or monkfish fillets

3 tablespoons olive oil

3 garlic cloves, crushed

1½ teaspoons ground cumin

1 teaspoon paprika

1 fresh green chilli, finely chopped

handful of coriander leaves, finely chopped

4 tablespoons lemon juice

salt

lemon wedges, to serve

1 Place the fish fillets in a shallow non-metallic dish. Mix together the olive oil, garlic, ground cumin, paprika, green chilli, chopped coriander, lemon juice and salt and pour over the fish. Cover and leave in a cool place for 3–4 hours, turning occasionally.

2 Put the fish fillets under a preheated grill and cook for about 4 minutes on each side, basting occasionally with the coriander mixture, until the flesh flakes when tested with the point of a sharp knife.

3 Serve warm with lemon wedges.

Serves 4

fragrant baked sea bream

1 tablespoon flaked almonds, lightly toasted and chopped

1 teaspoon paprika

1 teaspoon ground cinnamon

2 teaspoons ground cumin

pinch of crushed saffron threads

½ teaspoon cayenne pepper

2 garlic cloves, crushed

2 teaspoons caster sugar

750 g (1½ lb) sea bream, prepared

3 tablespoons lemon juice

4 tablespoons olive oil

salt and pepper

chopped coriander, to garnish

1 Mix together the almonds, paprika, cinnamon, cumin, saffron, cayenne pepper, garlic, sugar and season with salt and pepper. Cut 3 slashes in both sides of the sea bream. Rub the spice mixture over the fish, working it well into the slashes. Pour over the lemon juice and olive oil. Cover and leave in a cool place for 1 hour.

2 Put the fish and any marinade in a shallow earthenware baking dish, cover with foil and bake in a preheated oven, 180°C (350°F), Gas Mark 4, for about 20–25 minutes, depending on the thickness of the fish, until the flesh flakes when tested with a fork.

3 Serve on a bed of coriander sprigs and tomato slices.

Serves 2

bream in a couscous jacket, with tomato & mint salad

Couscous makes a crisp, nutty coating that keeps the breams' flesh beautifully succulent and locks in the flavour.

1 First make the salad. Stir together the garlic, lime juice, vinegar and half of the olive oil. Season with salt and pepper then add the tomatoes and half of the mint and gently toss together. Cover and refrigerate.

2 Mix together the couscous, almonds, spring onion, the remaining mint and plenty of black pepper and a little salt.

3 Dip each fish into the beaten egg, then coat evenly with the couscous mixture.

4 Heat the remaining olive oil in a large, preferably non-stick, frying pan. Add the fish in a single layer and fry for about 7 minutes on each side until the flesh flakes when tested with the point of a knife. Serve immediately with the tomato and mint salad.

Serves 4

40 g (1½ oz) fine couscous

20 g (¾ oz) blanched almonds, finely chopped

1 spring onion, thinly sliced

4 sea bream, each weighing about 250 g (8 oz), cleaned and scaled

1 large egg, beaten

salt and pepper

Tomato and Mint Salad:

1 plump garlic clove, crushed

1 teaspoon lime juice

1 teaspoon white wine vinegar

5 tablespoons olive oil

2 large sun-ripened tomatoes, skinned, deseeded and chopped

25 g (1 oz) mint, chopped

braised bream with vegetables & spices

This is a classic Moroccan way of cooking fish, on a bed of vegetables for the threefold purpose of flavouring it, keeping it moist and preventing it sticking to the dish.

1 Heat the oil in a large flameproof casserole, add the onion, garlic, carrots and fennel and cook gently until they begin to colour. Stir in the coriander, cumin, cloves and saffron and cook for 2 minutes. Put the fish on top of the vegetable mixture and pour on the stock. Season with salt and pepper and heat to simmering point.

2 Cover the casserole and transfer to a preheated oven, 160°C (325°F), Gas Mark 3, for 25–30 minutes until the fish just flakes when tested with a fork.

3 Taste the cooking liquid; if you feel it needs to be concentrated, transfer the fish and vegetables to a warmed serving platter and boil the liquid until it has reduced.

Serves 2–3

2 tablespoons olive oil

1 large onion, chopped

2 garlic cloves, crushed

2 small carrots, finely chopped

1 small fennel bulb, finely chopped

1 teaspoon ground coriander

½ teaspoon ground cumin

½ teaspoon ground cloves

small pinch of crushed saffron threads

1 kg (2 lb) sea bream, prepared

300 ml (½ pint) fish stock

salt and pepper

fish in golden marinade

In this recipe the fish is steeped in a fragrant, golden marinade after cooking. This was done originally in order to extend its storage time in the absence of refrigeration.

1 First make the marinade: heat the oil, add the onions and cook for 2 minutes. Add the cumin seeds and chilli flakes and stir for about 45 seconds. Add the red peppers and fry, stirring occasionally, until soft, then add the saffron and its liquid, orange rind and juice and lemon juice. Bubble for a few minutes, then add sugar and salt and pepper to taste. Leave to cool.

2 Coat the fish in the seasoned flour, then fry in the oil for about 2–3 minutes on each side, until browned and just cooked through.

3 Using a fish slice, transfer the fish to a shallow non-metallic dish. Leave to cool, then pour over the cooled marinade. Cover the dish, place in the refrigerator and leave the fish for 4–12 hours, turning it carefully 2–3 times.

4 Return the fish to room temperature about 30 minutes before serving garnished with coriander or parsley.

Serves 4 as a main course, 6–8 as a first course

6–8 sea bream fillets, scaled with the skin left on

3 tablespoons seasoned white flour

3 tablespoons virgin olive oil

chopped coriander or parsley, to garnish

Marinade:

3 tablespoons virgin olive oil

2 red onions, thinly sliced

1½ teaspoons cumin seeds, lightly crushed

½ teaspoon dried red chilli flakes

2 red peppers, cored, deseeded and sliced

large pinch of saffron threads, crushed and soaked in 3 tablespoons water

finely shredded rind and juice of 1 orange

2–3 tablespoons lemon juice

caster sugar, to taste

salt and pepper

prawns in chillied tomato sauce

The prawns for this recipe should be firm, fresh and flavourful so do not use the small frozen ones that ooze water when cooked otherwise you will have a disappointing dish.

1 Heat the oil in a heavy frying pan. Add the onions, garlic, chilli and lemon rind and fry briskly for 1–2 minutes. Add the tomatoes and fish stock, bring to the boil then simmer for 5 minutes.

2 Add the prawns, season with salt and pepper and cook, turning occasionally, for about 4 minutes until the prawns change colour. Sprinkle with the mixed herbs and serve straight away.

Serves 4

2 tablespoons olive oil

2 red onions, finely chopped

3 garlic cloves, crushed

1 fresh red chilli, deseeded and chopped

2 strips of lemon rind

2 large, ripe, well-flavoured ridged tomatoes, deseeded and chopped

150 ml (5 fl oz) fish stock

500 g (1 lb) large peeled raw prawns

2 tablespoons chopped mixed parsley and dill

salt and pepper

spiced sea bass

It would be more traditional to make this recipe using a whole fish and to cook it on top of the stove, but I have taken the liberty of adapting it to Western ways. The fillets can also be baked in individual greaseproof or foil parcels with one quarter of the spice mixture added to each one.

1 Put the fish in a shallow earthenware or non-metallic baking dish.

2 Mix together the olive oil, garlic, coriander, parsley, paprika, cumin, ground coriander, lemon juice and salt and pepper and pour over the fish. Turn the steaks over, cover and leave in a cool place for 1 hour.

3 Turn the steaks over again and cover the dish. Cook in a preheated oven, 220°C (425°F), Gas Mark 7, for 8–12 minutes until the fish flakes when tested with a fork.

Serves 4

4 sea bass fillets, each weighing about 175 g (6 oz)

2 tablespoons virgin olive oil

2 garlic cloves, crushed

2 tablespoons chopped coriander

2 tablespoons chopped parsley

2 teaspoons paprika

½ teaspoon ground cumin

½ teaspoon ground coriander

juice of ½ lemon

salt and pepper

red mullet with almond chermoula

Chermoula is the distinctive Moroccan mixture of coriander, garlic, chillies and spices that is used in many ways, bringing character and flavour to dishes. Its most frequent use is as a marinade, either before cooking or afterwards, for fish, grilled or baked meat, poultry, and vegetable dishes. The food may also be cooked in chermoula. Every cook has their own blend of ingredients, or more likely, blends, because the proportions and even the combinations of ingredients often vary according to the recipe being made.

1 Put the coriander, mint, almonds, garlic and chilli into a food processor or blender. With the motor running, slowly pour in the oil to make a coarse or smooth paste, according to taste. Season with salt and pepper and lemon juice.

2 With the point of a sharp knife, cut 2 deep slashes in both sides of each fish. Spread the chermoula over both sides of the fish, working it well into the slashes. Cover and leave in a cool place for 1 hour.

3 Put the mullet under a preheated grill and cook for 4–5 minutes on each side until the flesh just flakes when tested with a fork; adjust the distance from the grill to prevent the fish burning.

Serves 4

50 g (2 oz) fresh coriander

large handful of mint, roughly chopped

40 g (1½ oz) almonds

2 plump garlic cloves

pinch of dried chilli flakes

about 125 ml (4 fl oz) virgin olive oil

4 red mullet, each weighing 300 g (10 oz)

lemon juice

salt and pepper

chermoula with preserved lemon

This is another version of chermoula with the distinctive North African flavour of preserved lemon rind.

1 Put all the ingredients into a glass or pottery bowl and stir together. Cover and leave in a cool place, preferably not the refrigerator, for 2 hours.

1 Preserved Lemon (see page 102), rind only, finely chopped

2 plump garlic cloves, crushed

pinch of dried chilli flakes

bunch of parsley, chopped

½ teaspoon paprika

pinch of saffron threads

5 tablespoons olive oil

2 tablespoons lemon juice

1–2 tablespoons water

barbecued marinated sardines

Sardines take excellently to being cooked over a charcoal fire. The appetizing spicy-woody, slightly charred smell of these plump fish cooking over glowing embers, until their skins are flecked with black, is one of my over-riding memories of evenings spent along Morocco's coast. If the fish are less than about 13 cm (5 inches) long there is no need to gut them. Turning the fish over during cooking will be much easier if you use a wire fish basket.

1 To make the marinade, mix all the ingredients together in a jug or bowl.

2 Put the sardines into a glass or pottery dish. Pour over the marinade, turn the fish so that they are thoroughly covered in the marinade then cover the dish and leave in a cool place for 1 hour.

3 Remove the sardines from the marinade and cook over a preheated barbecue for 3–4 minutes on each side.

Serves 6

1 kg (2 lb) sardines

Marinade:

1½ tablespoons chopped fresh coriander

1½ tablespoons chopped parsley

3 garlic cloves, crushed

1 teaspoon ground cumin

1 teaspoon ground coriander

2 teaspoons paprika

pinch of crushed saffron threads (optional)

pinch of dried chilli flakes

finely grated rind and juice of 1 lemon

3 tablespoons virgin olive oil

salt

tunisian grilled sardines with tomato relish

With one of the richest and most diverse catches of fish in the Mediterranean, it's not surprising that Tunisians have a way with fish dishes.

1 Using the back of a knife, descale the sardines. Cut off the fins with scissors and slit along the stomach. Remove and discard the intestines. Wash the fish thoroughly, pat dry with kitchen paper and place in a shallow non-metallic dish.

2 To make the marinade, using a pestle and mortar pound together the garlic, coriander seeds and chilli with a pinch of salt. Add the lime rind and juice, then gradually work in the oil. Pour over the sardines, coat well with the mixture, then cover and leave for about 1 hour, turning the sardines 2–3 times.

3 Blend all the relish ingredients in a food processor or blender. Place the sardines on a barbecue or under a hot grill and cook for 2–3 minutes on each side, basting with the marinade.

4 Serve the sardines with the relish and garnish with coriander sprigs, if liked.

Serves 4

Variation: Sardines with Lemon and Coriander
Mix together 6 tablespoons olive oil, 3 tablespoons lemon juice, 2 tablespoons chopped fresh coriander and salt and pepper. Brush the mixture over 1 kg (2 lb) prepared fresh sardines, then cover and marinate for 1 hour. Cook the fish under a preheated grill for 2–3 minutes on each side, brushing with the lemon mixture as the fish browns and when turning it. Serve with the remaining lemon mixture poured over, and lemon wedges.

16 fresh sardines

sprigs of coriander, to garnish (optional)

Marinade:

1 garlic clove

2 teaspoons coriander seeds, toasted

1 dried red chilli, deseeded and chopped

finely grated rind and juice of 1 lime

4 tablespoons virgin olive oil

salt and pepper

Tomato relish:

4 spring onions, white part only, chopped

juice of 1 lime

250 g (8 oz) well-flavoured tomatoes, skinned, deseeded and chopped

½ sun-dried tomato, chopped

½ dried red chilli, deseeded and chopped

3 tablespoons chopped fresh coriander

moroccan prawns with spices

500 g (1 lb) raw tiger prawns
in their shells

4 tablespoons olive oil

2 garlic cloves, crushed

1 teaspoon ground cumin

½ teaspoon ground ginger

1 teaspoon paprika

¼ teaspoon cayenne pepper

leaves from a bunch of coriander,
finely chopped

salt

lemon wedges, to serve

Whenever I cook this dish my mind flies back to a glorious evening when I was sitting beneath a deep royal blue Tangier sky, the sleepy sounds of night drawing in, and the exotic aroma of prawns being cooked in this way wafting tantalizingly under my nose. The prawns can also be butterflied (use scissors to cut them lengthways almost in half, leaving the tails intact), then marinated in the spice mixture before grilling for 3–4 minutes; brush with any remaining marinade during cooking.

1 Remove the shells, legs, heads and entrails from most of the prawns, leave a few whole as they look attractive. Cut along the backs with the point of a sharp knife and remove the dark thread.

2 Heat the olive oil in a frying pan, add the garlic and cook until it becomes aromatic. Stir in the cumin, ginger, paprika and cayennne pepper, heat for about 30 seconds, then add the prawns. Fry quickly, stirring, until they turn pink. Stir in the coriander and season with salt, heat for about 30 seconds, then serve the prawns with the cooking juices spooned over and accompanied by lemon wedges.

Serves 4

squid with vegetable tagine

The vegetables are cooked first then the squid is quickly fried over a high heat at the last minute, because it quickly becomes tough if overcooked.

1 Heat 2 tablespoons of the olive oil in a large frying pan. Add the onion, garlic and chilli and cook until softened but not brown. Stir in the anchovy fillets, if using, mashing them so they dissolve.

2 Add the aubergine to the pan and cook for 5 minutes, stirring occasionally, then add the mint, parsley, thyme and courgettes. When the courgettes start to wilt add the peppers and tomatoes. Cook, stirring occasionally, until all the vegetables are tender.

3 Just before serving, heat the remaining oil in another large frying pan. Add the squid and fry over a high heat, stirring, for about 1 minute. Remove with a slotted spoon and add to the vegetables. Season to taste with salt and pepper and serve at once.

Serves 6

4 tablespoons virgin olive oil

2 onions, chopped

3 garlic cloves, crushed

1 fresh red chilli, deseeded and chopped

2 anchovy fillets (optional)

1 aubergine, weighing about 250 g (8 oz), cut into 2.5 cm (1 inch) cubes

2 tablespoons torn mint leaves

2 tablespoons chopped parsley

2 thyme sprigs

2 courgettes, sliced

2 red peppers, roasted and peeled if liked, cored, deseeded and thickly sliced

4 well-flavoured tomatoes, seeded and quartered

1 kg (2 lb) squid, prepared and cut into small squares

salt and pepper

mackerel marinated in chermoula

Mackerel seems too mundane a fish to have a place in Moroccan cooking, but in Tangiers fish market you will find it alongside the more exotic Mediterranean fish, some that are recognisable while others are a mystery. Being a strongly flavoured fish, mackerel takes easily to the spicing of this chermoula, and becomes an altogether more exciting fish.

3 garlic cloves

2 teaspoons ground cumin

2 teaspoons paprika

pinch of dried chilli flakes

small bunch of coriander, chopped

150 ml (¼ pint) olive oil

juice of 1 lemon

4 medium mackerel, cleaned

salt

lemon halves, to serve

1 Crush the garlic with a pinch of salt then work in the cumin, paprika, chilli flakes and coriander. Slowly add the oil, mixing it in thoroughly. Stir in the lemon juice.

2 Cut 3 or 4 slanting slashes in both sides of each fish. Spread the garlic mixture over the fish, working it well into the slashes. Place the fish in a shallow glass or pottery dish, cover and leave in a cool place for 1 hour.

3 Cook the fish under a preheated grill, or on a hot barbecue, turning once or twice, until the flesh just flakes when tested with a fork.

4 Serve with lemon halves.

Serves 4

mixed seafood tagine

750 g (1½ lb) mussels, thoroughly cleaned

1 onion, finely chopped

250 ml (8 fl oz) fish stock

2 ripe well-flavoured tomatoes, deseeded and chopped

1 whole garlic bulb, peeled and thinly sliced

¼ teaspoon ground cardamom

¼ teaspoon ground cumin

¼ teaspoon ground coriander

large pinch of ground allspice

large pinch of ground turmeric

250 g (8 oz) squid, prepared

250 g (8 oz) large raw prawns, peeled

salt and cayenne pepper

coriander sprigs, to garnish

As elsewhere around the Mediterranean, Moroccan fishermen, or rather their wives, make tagines from the best fresh fish that is available – a policy we should follow as often as possible in our own cooking.

1 Put the mussels, onion and stock into a large saucepan. Cover and cook over a medium heat, shaking the pan occasionally, for 3–5 minutes, depending on the size of the mussels, until they have all opened. Discard any that remain closed. Leave the mussels to cool before removing them from their shells. Set aside.

2 Strain the cooking liquid into a bowl, leave to stand for 2–3 minutes then carefully strain most of it into a large, heavy frying pan, leaving any sediment and the onion behind.

3 Add the tomatoes, garlic, cardamom, cumin, coriander, allspice and turmeric to the frying pan. Bring to the boil then simmer gently for about 5 minutes until the garlic is tender.

4 Add the squid to the pan, cover and poach for 1 minute until the pieces of squid curl up. Add the prawns, cover the pan and continue to cook gently for 1 further minute. Add the mussels, season with salt and cayenne pepper and cook for one further minute to heat through. Serve at once garnished with coriander sprigs.

Serves 4

meat

Lamb is far and away the most frequently eaten meat. Islam forbids the eating of pork, while much of the terrain and climate is unsuitable for cattle, and goats are kept for their milk rather than for eating. Traditionally in the desert very young lambs were sometimes killed for roasting whole on a spit, often for a celebration or festival. Such lamb is still prepared in this way, though in cities and towns it is more likely to be in the form of a joint (see page 62). Succulent kebabs and keftas, made fragrant and tasty with spices and charcoal smoke, are grilled on skewers over open fires, while tougher meat from older animals is transformed into morsels that are so tender they can be broken apart with bread by gentle coaxing in a tagine.

stuffed baked lamb

This is a magnificent dish for when you are catering for a large number of people. It is in the tradition of true Moroccan hospitality to prepare a large meal when serving many people.

1 First make the stuffing. Put the couscous into a bowl, pour over the boiling water, stir then leave until the water has been absorbed.

2 Heat a small heavy pan, add the coriander and cumin seeds and heat until fragrant. Grind to a powder then mix with the cinnamon.

3 Heat 1 tablespoon of the oil in a frying pan, add the pine nuts and almonds and fry until browned. Transfer to kitchen paper to drain. Add the remaining oil to the pan. When it is hot, add the onion and fry until soft. Stir in the garlic and spice mixture and fry for 2 minutes, then add the nuts, mint, coriander, raisins and salt and pepper.

4 Open out the lamb, skin side down, on a work surface. Season inside with pepper then spread over the stuffing. If possible, tuck the flaps of the piece of lamb over the stuffing. Roll up the lamb into a neat sausage shape then tie securely with string.

5 Preheat the oven to its highest setting. Put the chopped onion into a roasting tin that the lamb will just fit. Put the lamb on the onion and pour over the oil and lemon juice. Bake for 15 minutes then lower the oven temperature to 220°C (425°F), Gas Mark 7 and bake for a further 25 minutes so the lamb is pink in the centre. Remove the lamb from the oven, cover and leave to stand in a warm place for about 15 minutes before carving. Young green beans make an attractive accompaniment.

Serves 8–10

2 kg (4 lb) boned leg of lamb

1 onion, cut into thick wedges

3 tablespoons olive oil

juice of 2 lemons

Stuffing:

50 g (2 oz) couscous

150 ml (¼ pint) boiling water

2 teaspoons coriander seeds

2 teaspoons cumin seeds

1 teaspoon ground cinnamon

3 tablespoons olive oil

50 g (2 oz) pine nuts

50 g (2 oz) flaked almonds

1 large onion, finely chopped

2 garlic cloves, crushed

1 teaspoon dried mint

4 tablespoons chopped coriander leaves

50 g (2 oz) raisins

salt and pepper

mini mechoui

Mechoui is one of the great dishes of the Moroccan bled (countryside). It involves spit-roasting a whole lamb over an open fire. In some areas of Morocco, the lamb is cooked inside a beehive-shaped mud oven which is tightly sealed to retain the heat, while in others it is cooked over a slow-burning charcoal fire in a sealed pit.

1 Mix all the marinade ingredients together and rub over the lamb. Cover and leave in a cool place for at least 8 hours, turning the lamb occasionally.

2 Put the lamb on a spit or a rack over a roasting tin and cook in a preheated oven, 240°C (475°F), Gas Mark 9, for 15 minutes. Lower the heat to 180°C (350°F), Gas Mark 4 and roast for 18–20 minutes per pound or until cooked to your liking, turning the lamb frequently if it is cooked on a rack, until the meat can easily be removed from the bones with the fingers.

3 Transfer the lamb to a warm place, cover and leave to stand for 15 minutes.

4 Serve the lamb on a large platter accompanied by warm bread and saucers filled with salt and ground cumin or cumin seeds. Guests should remove the lamb from the joint with their fingers and dip it in the salt and cumin before eating.

Serves 6

1 leg of lamb, weighing about 2 kg (4 lb)

Marinade:

4 tablespoons olive oil

2 garlic cloves, crushed

5 cm (2 inch) piece of fresh root ginger, peeled and grated

4 teaspoons ground coriander

2 teaspoons ground cumin

1 teaspoon ground cinnamon

1 teaspoon ground cloves

pepper

To serve:

salt

ground cumin or cumin seeds

souk-grilled lamb

For this version of kebabs, rather than marinating the lamb with spices so their flavour permeates through the meat, the spices are sprinkled on to the lamb immediately it comes from the hot barbecue or grill so that you get a burst of spice as you bite into the kebab.

1 Put the lamb in a bowl. Mix together the onion, garlic, olive oil, salt and pepper. Add to the lamb, stir to mix well then cover and leave in a cool place for 1–2 hours.

2 Meanwhile, toast the cumin seeds in a dry heavy frying pan until fragrant, then grind to a powder.

3 Thread the lamb on to 3–4 skewers and cook under a preheated grill for about 4 minutes on each side until crisp and brown on the outside but still pink in the centre. Sprinkle the ground cumin and paprika over the lamb and serve straight away.

Serves 3–4

500 g (1 lb) shoulder of lamb, cut into large cubes

1 small onion, very finely chopped

2 garlic cloves, crushed

2 tablespoons olive oil

1 tablespoon cumin seeds

paprika, for sprinkling

salt and pepper

barbecued lamb

This is another example of the food that is so good in Morocco. There the lamb would be cooked over a charcoal fire, which means out of doors. Our summers do not allow this to be done very often and I've found a hot, heavy ridged grill pan is the best substitute when I want to enjoy these moreish chops in our chillier climate.

1 Place the chops in a shallow glass or pottery dish. Mix together the oil, onion, garlic, lemon juice, coriander, parsley, paprika, cumin and cayenne pepper. Pour the marinade evenly over the lamb and turn the chops to coat them evenly. Cover and leave in a cool place for 2 hours.

2 Lift the lamb from the marinade and pat dry. Cook the chops on a hot barbecue, a heated, dry, ridged grill pan or under a hot grill for 4 minutes on each side until lightly charred on the outside but still pink in the centre. Sprinkle with salt and serve.

Serves 4

4 chump chops

6 tablespoons olive oil

1 onion, grated

2 garlic cloves, crushed

juice of 1 lemon

3 tablespoons chopped fresh coriander

3 tablespoons chopped parsley

1 teaspoon paprika

1 teaspoon ground cumin

pinch of cayenne pepper

salt

smothered lamb

In this recipe, the lamb is sandwiched between two layers of sweet, succulent rich tasting onions. Use large onions because they have a sweeter, milder flavour than small ones and cook down better.

1 Heat the oil in a large frying pan, add the onions, season with salt and pepper and fry slowly until soft and golden. Stir in the garlic when the onions are nearly done.

2 Meanwhile, heat a small, dry heavy pan, add the cumin and coriander seeds and the cloves and fry until fragrant. Grind to a powder. Add the ground spices to the cooked onion mixture and spread half of the onion mixture in a heavy flameproof casserole. Transfer the remainder to a bowl.

3 Brown the chops in the frying pan then put them in the casserole. Cover with the remaining onions and pour over the tomatoes and their juice.

4 Stir the stock or water into the tomato paste then add to the casserole. Cover and cook over a low heat for 1 hour until the lamb is tender. Uncover the casserole towards the end of cooking if there is too much liquid. Season with salt and pepper and stir in the coriander leaves just before serving.

Serves 4

2 tablespoons olive oil

500 g (1 lb) large onions, sliced

5 garlic cloves, crushed

1 tablespoon cumin seeds

2 teaspoons coriander seeds

3 cloves

8 lamb cutlets or small chops

400 g (13 oz) can chopped tomatoes

150 ml (¼ pint) chicken or vegetable stock or water

2 tablespoons sun-dried tomato paste

large handful of coriander leaves

salt and pepper

lamb tagine with honeyed prunes

Although there is some similarity between the ingredients of this dish and those in Lamb Tagine with Celery & Prunes on the opposite page and Lamb Tagine with Squash & Chickpeas on page 74, the results are completely different. None is better than the other two; each has its own special character and charm.

1 Put the lamb into a bowl. Add the onions, garlic, oil, chilli flakes, ginger, cumin, paprika, saffron and plenty of black pepper. Stir to coat the meat well. Cover and leave to marinate in a cool place for at least 2 hours, or in the refrigerator overnight.

2 Heat a large, heavy frying pan. Add the lamb in batches and brown evenly. Transfer to a tagine or heavy casserole. Put the marinade into the frying pan and cook, stirring, for 2–3 minutes then stir into the lamb. Add the tomatoes, orange rind, cinnamon and half of the coriander. Mix well then cover and cook in a preheated oven, 160°C (325°F), Gas Mark 3, for 1¼ hours.

3 Meanwhile, put the prunes into a saucepan with the honey and just enough water to cover and simmer for 10 minutes.

4 Add the prunes and the cooking juices to the tagine and cook for 15 minutes, adding the remaining coriander after about 7 minutes.

5 Serve the tagine with the almonds scattered over and garnished with mint leaves.

Serves 6

1 kg (2 lb) shoulder of lamb, in 4 cm (1½ inch) cubes

2 Spanish onions, coarsely grated

3 plump garlic cloves, crushed

4 tablespoons olive oil

large pinch of dried chilli flakes

½ teaspoon ground ginger

½ teaspoon ground cumin

½ teaspoon paprika

pinch of crushed saffron threads

2 x 400 g (13 oz) cans tomatoes

1 strip orange rind

2 cinnamon sticks

bunch of coriander, chopped

24 large ready-to-eat prunes

3–4 tablespoons clear honey

75 g (3 oz) toasted blanched whole almonds

pepper

mint leaves, to garnish

lamb tagine with celery & prunes

2 tablespoons olive oil

1 teaspoon ground ginger

1 teaspoon ground coriander

1 cinnamon stick, broken in half

1.5 kg (3 lb) boneless shoulder or leg of lamb, cut into large cubes

450 ml (¾ pint) chicken or vegetable stock

2 tablespoons chopped parsley

2 tablespoons chopped celery leaves

1 Spanish onion, finely chopped

3 garlic cloves, crushed

2 celery sticks, thinly sliced

250 g (8 oz) ready-to-eat prunes

2 tablespoons clear honey

salt and pepper

toasted flaked almonds, to serve

In this method of making a tagine, the spices are fried with the lamb so that their flavour is seared into the meat.

1 Heat the oil in a large, heavy flameproof casserole. Add the ginger, coriander and cinnamon and stir over a low heat until they smell fragrant. Stir in the lamb until it is thoroughly coated with the spiced oil then cook gently for 10–15 minutes until it is lightly browned.

2 Pour in the stock, add the parsley and celery leaves and heat to simmering point. Cover tightly and cook very gently for 1 hour.

3 Add the onion, garlic, celery, prunes and honey, cover the casserole again and cook, stirring occasionally, for 1½ hours, removing the lid for the last 20 minutes or so to allow the liquid to reduce.

4 To serve, season to taste with salt and pepper and sprinkle with the flaked almonds.

Serves 6–8

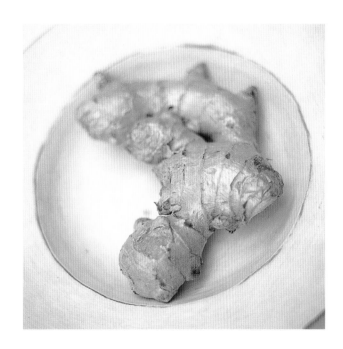

lamb with couscous

You can use this recipe as a starting point for many different versions. The lamb can be changed to chicken, or the meat can be left out altogether, and the vegetables can be altered or added to. The levels and types of spices can also be modified.

1 Put the lamb into a large saucepan. Add 900 ml (1½ pints) water, the onions, garlic, saffron, cinnamon, paprika, chilli, ginger and salt and pepper. Bring to the boil, remove the scum from the top, cover and simmer very gently for about 30 minutes. Add the carrots, turnips and kohlrabi or celeriac, cover and simmer for 15 minutes.

2 Put the couscous into a large bowl, pour over about 300 ml (½ pint) water, stir well and leave for 10 minutes. Add another 300 ml (½ pint) water and the oil and fork through the couscous to make sure the grains are separate, then leave for 10 minutes until swollen and tender but still separate. Put into a steamer and place, uncovered, over a saucepan of boiling water for about 10 minutes.

3 Meanwhile, add the courgettes and broad beans to the lamb. Add the tomatoes, coriander and parsley and cook for a further 5 minutes until the vegetables and lamb are tender.

4 Fork through the couscous to separate the grains, then turn on to a large serving plate. Dot the butter over the top, stir in and season with salt and pepper. Form into a mound with a large well in the centre and place the lamb in the well. Using a slotted spoon, lift the vegetables from the cooking broth and place on and around the lamb. Serve the remaining broth in a separate warmed bowl.

Serves 4

500 g (1 lb) lean lamb, cut into large cubes

2 onions, quartered then thickly sliced

2 garlic cloves, crushed

pinch of saffron threads, crushed

1 teaspoon ground cinnamon

½ teaspoon paprika

1 fresh red chilli, deseeded and finely chopped

½ teaspoon ground ginger

250 g (8 oz) small carrots, quartered lengthways

250 g (8 oz) small turnips, quartered

250 g (8 oz) kohlrabi or celeriac, cut into large chunks

500 g (1 lb) couscous

2 teaspoons olive oil

250 g (8 oz) courgettes, quartered lengthways

250 g (8 oz) broad beans

4 tomatoes, quartered

large bunch of coriander, chopped

large bunch of parsley, chopped

40 g (1½ oz) unsalted butter

salt and pepper

lalla's lamb

We get so used to browning the meat and vegetables before casseroling or braising them that it is easy to forget the much easier method of simply putting all the ingredients straight into a casserole and then starting the cooking. Lalla, who told me that she had been cooking since she was ten years old (at the time she must have been about 60) said that for this dish there was no point in spending time and effort browning the meat and vegetables. I have made this recipe both ways and I agree with her.

1 Put the lamb into a large bowl then stir in the onions, garlic, chilli, ginger, bay leaf and oil. Cover and leave in a cool place, not the refrigerator, for 4 hours. Alternatively, refrigerate overnight and return to room temperature 1 hour before cooking.

2 Stir the potatoes, aubergines, red peppers, tomatoes and their juice into the lamb and season with salt and pepper. Transfer to a casserole that the ingredients just fit, cover and bake in a preheated oven, 200°C (400°F), Gas Mark 6, for 30 minutes.

3 Lower the oven temperature to 160°C (325°F), Gas Mark 3 and cook for a further 1½ hours, stirring once or twice, until the lamb is very tender. If necessary, add a little water or stock to the casserole.

4 Scatter over the parsley and coriander before serving.

Serves 6

1 kg (2 lb) shoulder of lamb, cut into 5 cm (2 inch) cubes

750 g (1½ lb) large onions, thinly sliced

5 garlic cloves, crushed

1 fresh red chilli, deseeded and finely chopped

5 cm (2 inch) piece of fresh root ginger, peeled and grated

1 bay leaf, torn across

4 tablespoons olive oil

250 g (8 oz) potatoes, cut into 2.5 cm (1 inch) cubes

500 g (1 lb) small aubergines, cut into 2.5 cm (1 inch) cubes

2 red peppers, cored, deseeded and cut into strips

400 g (13 oz) can chopped tomatoes

salt and pepper

large handful of mixed parsley and coriander leaves, to garnish

lamb tagine with chickpeas & raisins

Vegetables and chickpeas are combined with lamb to make a nutritious, economical and sustaining dish, but fragrant spices make it a joy to eat so that you are not aware that you are eating such a virtuous meal. Instead of using chunks of lamb you could use 2 kg (4 lb) lamb shanks; cook them for 2 hours before adding the chickpeas and raisins.

1 Put the lamb into a deep bowl. Add the garlic, honey, olive oil, coriander, saffron, paprika, cumin and tomato paste and stir together. Season with salt and pepper, cover and leave in a cool place or the refrigerator overnight, stirring occasionally. If the lamb has been refrigerated, return it to room temperature 1 hour before cooking.

2 Put the meat and marinade into a roasting tin. Add the potatoes, carrots, shallots, stock and cinnamon and stir together. Cover with foil and bake in a preheated oven, 200°C (400°F), Gas Mark 6, for 1 hour.

3 Stir the chickpeas and raisins into the tagine and cook for 30 minutes. Remove the foil and cook for a further 30 minutes to brown the vegetables.

4 Serve the tagine garnished with coriander sprigs and accompanied by a small bowl of harissa.

Serves 6

1.75 kg (3½ lb) shoulder of lamb, with bone, cut into large pieces

6 plump garlic cloves, crushed

1 tablespoon clear honey

4 tablespoons olive oil

3 tablespoons chopped fresh coriander

pinch of crushed saffron threads

2 teaspoons paprika

2 teaspoons ground cumin

2 tablespoons sun-dried tomato paste

250 g (8 oz) potatoes, cut into chunks

250 g (8 oz) carrots, cut into chunks

250 g (8 oz) shallots, root ends intact

300 ml (½ pint) chicken or vegetable stock

2 cinnamon sticks

250 g (8 oz) can chickpeas, drained

250 g (8 oz) plump raisins

salt and pepper

coriander sprigs, to garnish

Harissa (see page 80), to serve

lamb b'stilla

Although b'stilla *traditionally has a pigeon or chicken filling, I have seen quite a number of other versions, such as mussel* b'stilla, b'stilla *with prawns and scallops, asparagus* b'stilla *and* b'stilla *with spiced lentils, and eaten some of them. This recipe, with red lentils and minced lamb, is a simplified version.*

1 Heat the oil in a saucepan. Add the onion and fry until transparent. Add the garlic, ginger, mint and paprika and stir for 1 minute, then add the lamb. Cook, stirring to break up the lumps, until the lamb changes colour. Mix in the lentils, tomato purée, harissa or chilli flakes, lemon juice, raisins and stock. Cover and cook very gently, stirring occasionally, for 20–25 minutes until the lentils are tender and most of the liquid has been absorbed. Uncover the pan, increase the heat slightly and let the liquid bubble, stirring frequently until the excess liquid has been driven off. Season with salt and pepper then pour into a bowl and leave to cool.

2 Oil a 23 cm (9 inch) shallow baking dish 3 cm (1¼ inch) deep. Line the dish with overlapping sheets of filo pastry, brushing each sheet with oil. There should not be any gaps in the pastry and the excess pastry should hang over the sides of the dish. Fill the dish with the lamb mixture. Fold the overhanging pastry over the lamb to cover the filling. Brush the top of the pastry with more oil and sprinkle over some poppy seeds.

3 Bake the pie in a preheated oven, 190°C (375°F), Gas Mark 5, for 30–35 minutes. Cover lightly with foil and continue to bake for a further 20 minutes. Allow the pie to cool for about 10 minutes before serving.

Serves 4

2 tablespoons olive oil, plus extra for brushing

1 onion, finely chopped

2 garlic cloves, crushed

2.5 cm (1½ inch) piece of fresh root ginger, peeled and grated

½ teaspoon dried mint

½ teaspoon paprika

250 g (8 oz) minced lean lamb

175 g (6 oz) red lentils

2 tablespoons tomato purée

Harissa (see page 80) to taste, or a pinch of dried chilli flakes

2 tablespoons lemon juice

50 g (2 oz) raisins

600 ml (1 pint) chicken or vegetable stock

about 125 g (4 oz) filo pastry, thawed if frozen

poppy seeds, for sprinkling

salt and pepper

braised mini keftas with eggs

To emulate the true character of this dish the eggs should be cooked with the yolks remaining runny so that when they are broken they flow over the keftas and merge with the tomato sauce, making a mild, creamy contrast to the spices. If possible, make the sauce and keftas a day in advance to allow the flavours to develop.

1 To make the sauce, put the oil, onion, garlic and tomatoes into a heavy pan and simmer, uncovered, stirring occasionally, until thick. Add the coriander towards the end of cooking. The sauce should have a pronounced flavour, so if necessary add sun-dried tomato paste, and season with chilli flakes, paprika and salt and pepper.

2 Heat a small, dry heavy frying pan, add the cumin seeds and fry until fragrant.

3 Put the onion, garlic, chilli and cumin seeds into a food processor and blend together. Add the meat, one of the eggs, the parsley and salt and pepper. Blend again until the mixture becomes a paste. Form into small balls between the size of a marble and a walnut.

4 Heat the oil, add the keftas and fry until just evenly browned on the outside. Put the keftas into the sauce and poach for 10 minutes.

5 Move the keftas and make 4 indentations in the sauce, using the back of a spoon. Break an egg carefully into each indentation, cover the pan and poach the eggs for about 8–10 minutes until lightly set. Sprinkle paprika over the eggs and serve at once.

Serves 4

4 teaspoons cumin seeds

1 onion, chopped

1 garlic clove, crushed

1 fresh red chilli, deseeded and chopped

500 g (1 lb) lamb, finely chopped

5 eggs

1 small bunch of parsley

oil, for frying

salt and pepper

Sauce:

4 tablespoons virgin olive oil

1 onion, finely chopped

2 garlic cloves, crushed

500 g (1 lb) ripe, well-flavoured tomatoes

2 tablespoons chopped coriander

sun-dried tomato paste (optional)

pinch of dried chilli flakes (optional)

paprika

lamb, artichoke & broad bean tagine

pinch of saffron threads

1 bunch of parsley

1 bunch of coriander

3 tablespoons olive oil or oil from the artichokes (see below)

1.5 kg (3 lb) leg or shoulder of lamb, cut into large chunks

1 onion, sliced

2 garlic cloves, crushed

250 ml (8 fl oz) stock or water

1 teaspoon ground coriander

1 teaspoon ground ginger

500 g (1 lb) jar artichokes in oil, drained

500 g (1 lb) frozen broad beans, thawed

2 Preserved Lemons (see page 102), rinds only, diced

pepper

coriander sprigs, to garnish

Artichokes in oil (which are now sold by many supermarkets) have a much better flavour and texture than canned artichokes. The oil left from the artichokes can be used in cooking, for tossing with pasta, rice or pulses and making salad dressings. If you can't get artichokes in oil, canned artichokes can be substituted but be sure to rinse them after draining.

1 Soak the saffron in the hot water. Tie the bunches of parsley and coriander together.

2 Heat the oil in a heavy flameproof casserole. Add the lamb in batches and fry until evenly browned. Transfer to kitchen paper to drain.

3 Stir the onion into the casserole and cook until softened and lightly browned, adding the garlic when the onion is almost ready. Return the meat to the casserole then pour in the stock or water and add the coriander, ginger, saffron and herbs. Cover the casserole tightly and cook gently, stirring occasionally, for about 1¼ hours or until the lamb is tender.

4 Stir the artichokes, broad beans and preserved lemon rinds into the casserole, cover and cook for a further 30 minutes. To serve, discard the bunches of herbs, season to taste and garnish with coriander sprigs.

Serves 6–8

lamb tagine with squash & chickpeas

This is a straightforward no-nonsense dish, but it is worth taking a little care when frying the lamb to make sure that it does fry and not simmer in its own juice.

1 Heat the oil in a saucepan. Add the lamb in batches and cook until evenly browned. Pour in the stock, add the cinnamon, cover the pan and simmer very gently for 1 hour.

2 Add the squash, onions or shallots, the lemon juice and honey, cover the casserole and simmer gently for 30 minutes until the vegetables are tender. Stir in the chickpeas and prunes and cook for a further 5 minutes. Season to taste and serve.

Serves 4

1 tablespoon olive oil

750 g (1½ lb) leg of lamb, cut into cubes

600 ml (1 pint) chicken stock

1½ teaspoons ground cinnamon

375 g (12 oz) butternut squash, cut into small cubes

250 g (8 oz) button onions or shallots, peeled with root ends left intact

3 tablespoons lemon juice

1 tablespoon clear honey

250 g (8 oz) cooked chickpeas

250 g (8 oz) ready-to-eat prunes

salt and pepper

lamb & fennel tagine

1 Heat 1 tablespoon of the oil in a heavy flameproof casserole. Add the fennel, onion and garlic and cook gently until softened and beginning to brown. Using a slotted spoon, transfer the vegetables to a plate.

2 Increase the heat and add the remaining oil to the casserole. When it is hot, stir in the lamb and cook, stirring frequently, until lightly browned. Add the coriander, cumin, ginger and chilli flakes, season with pepper and stir for 1 minute.

3 Return the fennel mixture to the casserole and stir in the stock or water. Heat to simmering point, then cover and cook very gently, stirring occasionally, for about 2 hours.

4 Stir in the raisins, cover the casserole, or leave it uncovered if there is a lot of liquid remaining, and cook for 15 minutes. Season to taste with salt and pepper and garnish with coriander.

Serves 4

2 tablespoons olive oil

1 fennel bulb, sliced

1 onion, chopped

2 garlic cloves, crushed

750 g (1½ lb) boneless shoulder or leg of lamb, cut into chunks

2 teaspoons ground coriander

2 teaspoons ground cumin

1 teaspoon ground ginger

pinch of dried chilli flakes

500 ml (17 fl oz) veal or vegetable stock, or water

50 g (2 oz) raisins

salt and pepper

coriander sprigs, to garnish

radia's lamb with rice

In the original version of this recipe the rice is cooked separately then formed into a pyramid on a large serving platter and the lamb, vegetables and sauce spooned on to it. I much prefer it the way Radia cooked it, in her modern flat in the heart of Casablanca, so the rice is impregnated with the aromatic flavours of the spices and the taste of the vegetables. If you cook the lamb without the rice you will only need about 450 ml (¾ pint) stock. This version of the recipe is illustrated in the background of the picture on page 76.

1 Put the lamb in a glass or pottery bowl. Add all the marinade ingredients and stir together. Cover and leave overnight in a cool place or the refrigerator. If you refrigerate it, return the lamb to room temperature 1 hour before cooking.

2 Heat the oil in a large flameproof casserole. Add the celery and red peppers and fry for 2–3 minutes. Remove with a slotted spoon and set aside.

3 Drain the marinade from the lamb, reserving the marinade. Add the lamb to the casserole in batches and fry for 3–4 minutes until an even light brown. Transfer to kitchen paper to drain.

4 Stir the onion into the casserole and cook until golden. Add the marinade and bubble for 2 minutes, then add the rice. Stir over a low heat for 1 minute then add the stock and tomatoes. Bring to the boil, stirring.

5 Return the lamb to the rice mixture and season generously with salt and pepper. Cover tightly and simmer very gently for 30 minutes.

6 Stir in the celery and red pepper, cover and cook for 10 minutes. Serve garnished with coriander and lemon.

Serves 8

1 kg (2 lb) boneless leg of lamb, cut into large cubes

2 tablespoons olive oil

125 g (4 oz) celery, sliced

2 red peppers, cored, deseeded and cut into strips

1 large onion, finely chopped

300 g (10 oz) white long-grain rice

900 ml (1½ pints) chicken or vegetable stock

400 g (13 oz) can tomatoes

salt and pepper

Marinade:

9 garlic cloves, crushed

5 tablespoons chopped fresh coriander

3 fresh red chillies, deseeded and chopped

large pinch of saffron threads

4½ teaspoons paprika

4½ teaspoons ground cumin

150 ml (¼ pint) olive oil

100 ml (3½ fl oz) lemon juice

To garnish:

coriander sprigs

lemon wedges

lamb & dried apricot tagine

Moroccans have a sweet tooth and the original recipe included honey. However I have left this out as I think the dried apricots have sufficient sweetness to give a well-balanced taste, but you may like to include a spoonful or two.

1 Heat the oil in a heavy flameproof casserole, add the lamb and cook until evenly browned. Transfer to a bowl. Stir the onion into the casserole and cook over a fairly low heat, stirring occasionally, until soft and beginning to colour. Stir in the garlic and ginger, increase the heat to moderate and cook for about 1 minute.

2 Add the celery, saffron, coriander and cumin and stir for 30 seconds, then return the lamb and any juices that have collected in the bowl to the casserole. Add salt and pepper and sufficient water just to cover the meat, cover the casserole tightly and cook gently for about 1 hour, stirring occasionally.

3 Stir the apricots and their soaking liquid, and the orange juice into the casserole, cover and cook for 30 minutes or so until all the ingredients are tender and the liquid is reduced and well flavoured. If there is too much liquid or it is too thin, transfer the meat and vegetables to a warmed serving dish and boil the liquid to concentrate it. Pour into the serving dish and stir the ingredients together. Garnish with chopped parsley.

Serves 4

3–4 tablespoons olive oil

625 g (1¼ lb) lean lamb, cubed

1 Spanish onion, finely chopped

3 garlic cloves, chopped

50 g (2 oz) fresh root ginger, peeled and finely chopped

2 celery sticks, thinly sliced

pinch of saffron threads, roasted and crushed

1 teaspoon coriander seeds, roasted and crushed

1 teaspoon cumin seeds, roasted and crushed

150 g (5 oz) dried apricots, soaked overnight just covered by water

juice of 1 orange

salt and pepper

chopped parsley, to garnish

lamb tagine with okra & almonds

1 Put the lamb, onion, garlic, red pepper, ginger, cinnamon, paprika, stock, honey and lemon juice into a heavy flameproof casserole and heat to just on simmering point. Cover the casserole tightly and cook for about 1¼ hours, stirring occasionally.

2 Add the okra and almonds. Cover the casserole or leave it uncovered if there is a lot of liquid left, and cook for a further 15–20 minutes until the okra is tender.

3 Season to taste and serve.

Serves 4

1 kg (2 lb) boneless shoulder or leg of lamb, cut into large cubes

1 onion, chopped

3 garlic cloves, crushed

1 large red pepper, cored, deseeded and sliced

5 cm (2 inch) piece of fresh root ginger, peeled and grated

2 teaspoons ground cinnamon

2 teaspoons paprika

600 ml (1 pint) veal or vegetable stock, or water

1½ tablespoons clear honey

juice of 1 lemon

375 g (12 oz) okra, trimmed

75 g (3 oz) whole blanched almonds

salt and pepper

lamb shanks in red juices

about 4 tablespoons olive oil

2 lamb shanks

2 small aubergines, halved lengthways and thickly sliced

2 large onions, sliced

4 garlic cloves, crushed

1 cinnamon stick

400 g (13 oz) can chopped tomatoes

2 tablespoons sun-dried tomato paste

2 teaspoons Harissa (see below)

salt and pepper

1 Heat 2 tablespoons of the oil in a heavy flameproof casserole. Add the lamb and brown evenly. Remove to a plate with a slotted spoon.

2 Add the remaining oil to the casserole and brown the aubergines in batches, adding more oil if necessary. Using a slotted spoon, transfer the aubergines to a plate.

3 Lower the heat slightly then add the onions and garlic to the casserole and cook until soft and lightly browned. Stir in the cinnamon stick, tomatoes, tomato paste and harissa then return the lamb and aubergines to the casserole. Add enough water to come almost to the top of the shanks. Heat to just on simmering point then cover tightly and cook very gently for about 1½–2 hours until the lamb is very tender.

4 Lift the lamb on to a warmed plate. Remove as much fat as possible from the top of the cooking juices. Boil the juices in the casserole until thickened and the flavour concentrated to your liking, season well, then spoon around the lamb.

Serves 2

harissa

Harissa is the fiery blend of red chillies, onions, garlic and spices that adds life to dishes. It is used during the preparation of dishes, and appears in small bowls on the table. It originated in Tunisia although it is now used throughout Morocco and Algeria as well.

1 Put the red peppers, the chillies and their seeds, garlic, coriander and caraway seeds and a pinch of salt in a food processor or blender and mix together, adding enough oil to make a thick paste.

2 Pack the harissa into a small, clean, dry jar and pour a layer of oil over the top. Cover with a tight-fitting lid and keep in the refrigerator.

2 red peppers, roasted and skinned

25 g (1 oz) fresh red chillies, chopped, seeds retained

1–2 garlic cloves, crushed

½ teaspoon coriander seeds, toasted

2 teaspoons caraway seeds

olive oil

salt

lamb & okra tagine

3 tablespoons vegetable oil

1 kg (2 lb) lean lamb, cubed

1 large onion, chopped

3 garlic cloves

1 teaspoon ground coriander

½ teaspoon ground cumin

500 g (1 lb) okra, trimmed

4 well-flavoured tomatoes, skinned, deseeded and chopped

1–2 tablespoons sun-dried tomato paste

lemon juice, to taste

salt and pepper

chopped parsley or coriander, to garnish

In this tagine, the lamb and okra are cooked with a different selection of spices from those used in the tagine on page 78 and the lamb is browned before the vegetables and spices are added.

1 Heat the oil in a heavy flameproof casserole, add the lamb in batches and cook until brown. Using a slotted spoon, transfer the lamb to a bowl.

2 Stir the onion and garlic into the casserole and cook, stirring occasionally, until lightly browned. Stir in the ground coriander and cumin, then add the okra and cook for a few minutes more. Stir in the tomatoes and tomato paste and enough lemon juice to taste and cook for a further 2–3 minutes.

3 Return the lamb to the casserole with any juices that have collected in the bowl. Add salt and pepper to taste, pour in sufficient water to almost cover the lamb and bring just to simmering point. Cover the casserole tightly and cook gently for about 1½ hours until the lamb is very tender; stir gently occasionally during cooking and add a little warm water if necessary, but at the end of cooking the sauce should be thick.

4 Serve sprinkled with parsley or coriander.

Serves 4–6

lamb, shallot & date tagine

Boiling the shallots for a short time makes the task of peeling them much easier. If you leave the root ends intact they will hold the shallots together during cooking. In Morocco there are many different types of dates, plump, juicy and each with its own particular flavour – a far cry from the dried, sweet dates packed in little wooden boxes that appear here at Christmas. Although we are unable to get the variety of dates that is available to Moroccan and North African cooks, we do now have good fresh dates, notably medjool, *which are the ones to use for this recipe, and other regional recipes that call for dates.*

1 Put the lamb into a large bowl. Mix together the coriander, ginger, saffron and 1 tablespoon of the oil and stir into the lamb so the meat is evenly coated. Cover and leave in the refrigerator overnight.

2 Next day, remove the lamb from the refrigerator 1 hour before cooking. Bring a saucepan of water to the boil, add the shallots and boil gently for 2 minutes. Drain the shallots, rinse under running cold water and leave them until cool enough to handle before peeling; leave the root ends intact.

3 Heat 1 further tablespoon of the oil in a heavy casserole, add the lamb in batches and cook until evenly browned; add more oil as necesary. Remove all the lamb from the casserole.

4 Put the garlic into the casserole and stir for 1 minute then add the lamb, flour, shallots, stock, tomato paste, cinnamon, coriander, parsley and bay leaf. Stir together and heat to simmering point. Cover the casserole tightly and cook gently, stirring occasionally, for 1¼ hours.

5 Add the dates and honey, season with salt and pepper and cook for 15 minutes. Depending on the amount of liquid remaining, cover the casserole or leave it uncovered.

Serves 6–8

1.5 kg (3 lb) boneless leg or shoulder of lamb, cut into large cubes

2 teaspoons ground coriander

2 teaspoons ground ginger

large pinch of crushed saffron threads

4 tablespoons olive oil

18 shallots

4 garlic cloves, crushed

1 tablespoon plain flour

600 ml (1 pint) chicken or vegetable stock

1 tablespoon sun-dried tomato paste

1 large cinnamon stick, broken in half

2 tablespoons chopped coriander

2 tablespoons chopped parsley

1 bay leaf, torn across

125 g (4 oz) pitted plump dates, halved lengthways

1 tablespoon clear honey

salt and pepper

poultry

Anyone who thinks that chicken is boring should take a look at what Moroccan cooks do with the bird; they would then soon realise how wrong they are. With imagination and ingenuity, hens appear on the table in innumerable guises, from simple grilled chicken, marinated before cooking to give it that special flavour, to sustaining dishes that include pulses such as chickpeas, and opulent tagines flavoured with saffron. Chicken is combined with plump fruits, with nuts and with all manner of vegetables, from aubergines to turnips. Spices in varying combinations, proportions and levels are often present, but not always. Chicken may also be used in the king of Moroccan poultry dishes, B'stilla (see page 99), although traditionally the bird used is pigeon. As in many other countries, turkey is cooked for special occasions and, again, Moroccan cooks manage to show how succulent and flavoursome it can be.

chicken tagine with almonds & saffron

The coriander that is scattered over the chicken as a garnish does more than make the dish look attractive, so should not be omitted; it makes a vital contribution to the flavour and character of the dish.

1 Heat the oil in a heavy flameproof casserole. Add the chicken and brown evenly. Transfer to kitchen paper to drain.

2 Add the onions, celery, carrots and garlic to the casserole and cook gently for 5–7 minutes until lightly coloured. Add the stock and saffron. Stir in the almonds, season with salt and pepper and bring to the boil. Return the chicken to the casserole and add enough water to almost cover. Heat to simmering point then cover the casserole tightly and cook very gently for about 30–40 minutes until the chicken juices run clear when the thickest part is pierced with the point of a sharp knife.

3 Remove the chicken to a warmed serving platter, cover and keep warm. Boil the cooking liquid to reduce it to the right consistency and flavour. Scatter over the coriander leaves and serve.

Serves 4

2 tablespoons olive oil

4 large chicken breasts

2 onions, very finely chopped

2 celery sticks, finely chopped

2 small carrots, very finely chopped

1 garlic clove, crushed

150 ml (¼ pint) chicken stock

large pinch of saffron threads

50 g (2 oz) almonds, freshly ground

salt and pepper

roughly chopped coriander leaves, to garnish

moroccan red chicken

1 Heat 25 g (1 oz) of the butter in a heavy flameproof casserole. Add the chicken in batches and brown evenly. Remove to kitchen paper to drain.

2 Add the onion to the casserole and fry gently until softened and translucent. Add the peppercorns, paprika, cumin and cinnamon then return the chicken pieces to the pan. Pour in enough water to just cover the chicken, cover the casserole tightly and simmer gently for about 1 hour, turning the chicken a couple of times.

3 Transfer the chicken to a warmed platter. Boil the cooking juices hard until reduced by half, then strain the juices and stir in the coriander and lemon juice. Season with salt to taste. Pour the juices over the chicken and serve.

Serves 4

75 g (3 oz) unsalted butter

4 chicken joints

1 onion, chopped

1 teaspoon black peppercorns, crushed

2 teaspoons paprika

1 teaspoon cumin seeds

5 cm (2 inch) cinnamon stick

1 tablespoon chopped fresh coriander

juice of 1 lemon

salt

chicken tagine
with aubergines

*This dish is a typical example of the style of cooking in which an aubergine is mashed and
simmered in the chicken cooking juices to make a thick sauce.*

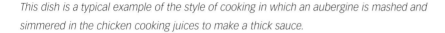

1 Put the chicken into a glass or pottery bowl. Put all the marinade ingredients into a
food processor or blender and mix together. Pour the marinade over the chicken, turning
the chicken over so that it is covered completely. Cover and refrigerate for about
8 hours, turning the chicken occasionally.

2 Bring the chicken to room temperature 1 hour before cooking.

3 Transfer the chicken and marinade to a heavy flameproof casserole and set it over
a low heat. Bring to simmering point, covered, then cook, tightly covered, for about
1½ hours, turning the chicken occasionally, until the juices run clear when the thickest
part of the chicken is pierced with a skewer.

4 Meanwhile, sprinkle the aubergine with salt and leave for 1 hour. Rinse well and dry
thoroughly. Heat the olive oil in a frying pan, add the aubergine, in batches if necessary,
and cook until tender and lightly browned. Remove to kitchen paper to drain.

5 Transfer the chicken to a warmed platter, cover and keep warm. Reserve a few slices
of aubergine for garnish. Add the remaining aubergines, the stock and lemon juice to the
cooking liquid in the casserole. Bring to the boil, mashing the aubergines with a fork, and
simmer to make a sauce. Taste and adjust the seasoning and pour the sauce over the
chicken. Garnish with the reserved aubergine slices and lemon wedges.

Serves 4

1.5 kg (3 lb) chicken

**2 aubergines, peeled and cut
into 1 cm (½ inch) slices**

4 tablespoons olive oil

125 ml (4 fl oz) chicken stock

2 tablespoons lemon juice

salt and pepper

lemon wedges, to garnish

Marinade:

2 onions, quartered

3 garlic cloves

small bunch of parsley

1 tablespoon ground ginger

1 teaspoon ground turmeric

pinch of crushed saffron threads

3 tablespoons olive oil

juice of 1 lemon

chicken, squash & sweet potato tagine

2 tablespoons olive oil

1.5 kg (3 lb) chicken, cut into
8 pieces

2 large onions, finely chopped

4 garlic cloves, crushed

2 cinnamon sticks, broken in half

500 g (1 lb) sweet potatoes, cut
into small cubes

500 g (1 lb) squash or pumpkin,
cut into small cubes

small handful of chopped mixed
parsley and mint

300 ml (½ pint) chicken or
vegetable stock

salt and pepper

flaked almonds, to garnish

Squash and sweet potatoes and just one spice, cinnamon, make this a mild, soothing tagine. Some of the parsley and mint are reserved to add at the end to give a bit of zip to the flavour, and flaked almonds are scattered over for a contrast in texture.

1 Heat the oil in a large heavy casserole. Add the chicken in batches and brown evenly. Remove and keep warm. Add the onions to the casserole and cook until soft and lightly browned, adding the garlic and cinnamon when the onions are nearly done.

2 Stir in the sweet potatoes and squash or pumpkin, then return the chicken to the pan, add half of the parsley and mint and pour in the stock. Cover tightly and simmer very gently for about 45 minutes until the chicken and vegetables are tender.

3 Season to taste with salt and pepper then add the remaining parsley and mint. Scatter over the almonds and serve.

Serves 4

chicken tagine with rice & chickpeas

125 g (4 oz) chickpeas, soaked overnight and drained

juice of 1 lemon

pinch of crushed saffron threads

2 tablespoons olive oil

4 chicken leg joints

2 large onions, chopped

2 large red peppers, cored, deseeded and thickly sliced lengthways

3 garlic cloves, crushed

1 fresh red chilli, deseeded and finely chopped

1½ teaspoons ground cumin

1½ teaspoons ground coriander

stalks from a bunch of coriander, chopped

1 ripe thin-skinned lemon, thinly sliced

175 g (6 oz) white long-grain rice

425 ml (15 fl oz) chicken stock

125 g (4 oz) mixed pitted green and black olives

salt and pepper

leaves from a bunch of coriander, to garnish

A traditional way of cooking rice in a tagine or kdra is inside a large muslin bag, the theory being that the rice absorbs the flavoured cooking liquid but does not stick to the pan. However, I've found that the rice is more likely to stick together when cooked in the bag. Also, I've never had a problem with rice sticking to the pan, and making and washing the bag is a bit of a nuisance.

1 Cook the chickpeas in boiling water for 20 minutes. Drain.

2 Put the lemon juice into a small bowl, add the saffron and leave to soak.

3 Heat the oil in a heavy flameproof casserole. Add the chicken in batches and brown quickly. Transfer to kitchen paper to drain. Add the onions and red peppers to the pan and cook over a high heat, stirring frequently, until browned. Lower the heat and stir in the garlic, chilli, cumin, ground coriander and coriander stalks, lemon slices, rice, chickpeas, saffron liquid and stock. Return the chicken to the casserole, heat to simmering point then cover and cook very gently for 30 minutes.

4 Scatter the olives over the casserole and push them into the liquid. Cover the casserole and cook for a further 30 minutes until the chickpeas, rice and chicken are tender.

5 Season to taste and strew the coriander leaves over the top before serving.

Serves 4–6

quick chicken with lemon & olives

There are two deviations from the usual Moroccan recipe for chicken with lemons and olives, which make this version relevant for modern quick cooking. The first is that the dish is cooked quickly rather than being simmered slowly for a long time, and the second is that it uses fresh lemons instead of preserved lemons. This is just as delicious but in a different way. For the authentic version see page 102.

1 Put the chicken thighs into a dish. Crush the garlic with a pinch of salt, the cumin, paprika and plenty of black pepper. Blend with half of the olive oil then spoon over the chicken and stir well to mix thoroughly. Cover and leave in a cool place to marinate for up to 4 hours.

2 Heat the remaining oil in a small, shallow, flameproof cassserole, add the chicken and brown evenly. Remove with a slotted spoon and drain on kitchen paper.

3 Add the onion to the pan and fry, stirring occasionally, until soft and golden. Add the saffron and stir for 1 minute, then return the chicken to the pan. Pour over the lemon juice and stock. Add the sliced lemon and heat to simmering point. Add the olives, cover the pan and adjust the heat so the liquid gives an occasional bubble. Cook for about 15–20 minutes, turning the chicken thighs over two or three times, until they are tender. If necessary, remove the chicken to a warmed serving platter and boil the cooking juices hard until reduced to a thick sauce. Spoon over the chicken.

Serves 2

6 small or 4 large chicken thighs

2 plump garlic cloves

2 teaspoons ground cumin

2 teaspoons paprika

4 tablespoons olive oil

1 onion, finely chopped

1 teaspoon saffron threads

juice of 1 large lemon

250 ml (8 fl oz) chicken stock

1 large lemon, sliced

125 g (4 oz) green olives, pitted

salt and pepper

chicken tagine with vegetables & chickpeas

2 tablespoons olive oil

1 Spanish onion, chopped

4 garlic cloves, crushed

1 fresh red chilli, deseeded and finely chopped

1 tablespoon grated fresh root ginger

1½ teaspoons ground cumin

1½ teaspoons ground coriander

1 teaspoon ground allspice

4 chicken leg joints

750 ml (1¼ pints) chicken stock

1 red pepper, cored, deseeded and sliced

1 courgette, sliced

2 carrots, sliced

375 g (12 oz) cooked chickpeas

heated couscous, to serve

chopped coriander, to garnish

1 Heat the oil in a saucepan. Add the onion, garlic, chilli and ginger and cook until the onion has softened and is lightly browned. Add the cumin, coriander and allspice and stir for 1 minute, then add the chicken. Pour in the stock and heat to simmering point. Cover and simmer gently for 30 minutes.

2 Add the red pepper, courgette and carrots. Cover the pan again and continue to simmer for 30 minutes until the vegetables are tender.

3 Add the chickpeas to the pan and simmer, uncovered, for 5 minutes.

4 Make a bed of couscous on a large, warmed serving dish. Put the chicken in the centre. Scoop the vegetables from the casserole using a slotted spoon and add to the chicken. Pour the cooking juices over the chicken and couscous. Scatter over the chopped coriander.

Serves 4

saffron chicken with apricots

400 g (13 oz) can chopped
tomatoes

1 small onion, chopped

1 garlic clove, crushed

175 g (6 oz) whole dried apricots

1.75 kg (3½ lb) chicken, jointed

2 teaspoons ground cinnamon, plus
extra for flavouring

pinch of crushed saffron threads

3 tablespoons lemon juice, plus
extra for flavouring

2 teaspoons orange flower water

1 tablespoon olive oil

50 g (2 oz) dried apricots, sliced

3 tablespoons flaked almonds

2 tablespoons raisins

salt and pepper

Orange flower water gives an unusual sweet, fragrant flavour to this recipe. The finish of the dish is a little more complicated than most of those in this book; the cooking juices are puréed to make a sauce, and it is garnished with fried dried apricots, raisins and almonds flavoured with cinnamon and lemon juice.

1 Make up the can of tomatoes to 450 ml (¾ pint) with water and pour half of it into a heavy casserole, then add the onion, garlic and the whole dried apricots. Put the chicken into the casserole.

2 Mix the remaining tomato mixture with the cinnamon, saffron and lemon juice and pour over the chicken. Heat to simmering point then cover the casserole tightly and simmer very gently for about 35 minutes.

3 Transfer the chicken to a warmed serving platter, cover and keep warm.

4 Pour the contents of the casserole into a food processor and blend to a purée. Strain the purée if you like. Pour the purée into a saucepan and add the orange flower water and season with salt and pepper.

5 Heat the oil in another saucepan, add the sliced dried apricots, the almonds and raisins. Toss to warm through then flavour with lemon juice and cinnamon.

6 Arrange the chicken joints in a warmed serving dish, pour over the sauce and scatter with the almond mixture. Serve with a salad.

Serves 4

spiced baked chicken

Moroccan cooks are more likely to cook a whole chicken than chicken joints, but the reverse is true in Britain, so I have modified the recipe slightly to suit our cooking. The recipe transforms ordinary, frozen chicken into a memorable, tasty meal.

1½ tablespoons paprika

1 tablespoon ground cumin

1½ teaspoons ground turmeric

½ teaspoon cayenne pepper

3 garlic cloves, crushed

6 tablespoons lemon juice

4–8 chicken pieces, depending on size

3 tablespoons olive oil

salt and pepper

1 Mix the paprika, cumin, turmeric, cayenne pepper, garlic, salt and pepper with the lemon juice. Rub into the chicken, pushing the spice mixture a little way under the chicken skin. Cover and leave in a cool place for 3 hours.

2 Put the chicken, skin-side down, in a shallow earthenware baking dish and spoon over any spice juices and the oil. Bake in a preheated oven, 200°C (400°F), Gas Mark 6, for about 20–25 minutes, basting occasionally, until the chicken is very tender and the juices run clear when the thickest part is pierced with the point of a sharp knife.

3 Transfer the chicken to a warmed serving platter and keep warm. Skim the fat from the cooking juices and boil the remainder until reduced and slightly syrupy. Pour the sauce over the chicken.

Serves 4

---

chicken with almonds, apricots & raisins

1 tablespoon olive oil

4 chicken portions

1 Spanish onion, chopped

2 garlic cloves, crushed

1 teaspoon ground cinnamon

large pinch of saffron threads, crushed

50 g (2 oz) whole blanched almonds

125 g (4 oz) ready-to-eat dried apricots

25 g (1 oz) raisins

600 ml (1 pint) chicken stock

salt and pepper

1 Heat the oil in a heavy flameproof casserole. Add the chicken and brown evenly. Transfer to a plate. Add the onion and garlic to the casserole and cook until softened but not browned. Stir in the cinnamon for 1 minute.

2 Add the saffron, almonds, apricots, raisins and stock. Heat until the stock is just simmering then cover the casserole tightly and cook gently for about 1 hour until the chicken juices run clear when the thickest part is pierced with a sharp knife. Season to taste and serve.

Serves 4

rabat chicken
with oranges

I have adapted this dish from an original Rabat recipe that involved poaching the chicken in a well-flavoured, tomatoey liquid then removing it from the liquid and browning the bird in copious amounts of butter. The cooking liquid was thickened with the chicken livers and boiled down to make a rich sauce. This version is much simpler and more suited to today's cooks and tastes; many people will find it more delicious because of this.

1 Put 2 of the orange segments into the chicken cavity. Season the bird with salt and pepper, brush with 1 tablespoon of the oil and place on one breast in a roasting tin. Bake in a preheated oven, 200°C (400°F), Gas Mark 6, for 20 minutes.

2 Heat the remaining oil in a saucepan, add the onion, garlic, cumin, ginger and cinnamon and cook, stirring frequently, until the onion has softened. Add the saffron, stock, tomatoes, almonds and honey, bring to the boil then simmer for 3–4 minutes.

3 Turn the chicken on to the other breast. Add the remaining orange segments and add the tomato sauce. Bake the bird for a further 20 minutes then turn it on its back and bake for another 35 minutes until the juices run clear when the thickest part is tested.

Serves 4–6

2 large well-flavoured oranges, peeled and divided into segments

1.5 kg (3 lb) chicken

3 tablespoons olive oil

1 onion, sliced

2 garlic cloves, crushed

2 teaspoons cumin seeds

2.5 cm (1 inch) piece of fresh root ginger, peeled and grated

1 cinnamon stick

pinch of crushed saffron threads

300 ml (½ pint) chicken stock

4 large tomatoes, skinned and chopped

125 g (4 oz) blanched whole almonds, toasted

3 tablespoons clear honey

salt and pepper

b'stilla

No book on Moroccan cooking would be complete without a recipe for b'stilla. *It is one of the great, grand dishes of the region, and traditionally it is a rather complicated one. For a start, it should be made using* ouarka *(see page 8), which is beyond most cooks. The filling can include quails, pigeons or chicken, which are jointed after cooking but the flesh is left on the bone. The eggs are over-cooked by our standards, being heated for so long that the water seeps from the coagulated mass; this is then left to drain. B'stilla is served really piping hot as a first course. The thumb and first two fingers of the right hand are plunged through the pastry crust into the steaming filling and the size mouthful required is pulled out and quickly transferred to the mouth.*

1 Put the chicken into a saucepan with the onion, ginger, saffron, coriander, 1 teaspoon of the cinnamon, parsley and season with salt and pepper. Add enough water to barely cover the bird and simmer gently, covered, for 45 minutes until the chicken is tender.

2 Transfer the chicken to a plate. Boil the cooking juices until they are reduced to a thick, dryish sauce.

3 When the chicken is cool enough to handle, remove the skin and take the flesh from the bones. Coarsely chop the flesh.

4 Beat the eggs and butter with half of the cooking juices and cook, stirring constantly, until scrambled.

5 Toast the almonds in a dry heavy frying pan, stirring frequently, until lightly browned. Add the remaining cinnamon and the sugar.

6 Using overlapping sheets of filo pastry and brushing each sheet with oil, make a square 3 layers thick and 46 cm (18 inches) across on a baking sheet. Spread the remaining cooking juices in an 18 cm (7 inch) circle in the centre of the pastry. Cover with the egg mixture then top with the chicken and the almonds. Fold up the sides of the pastry to enclose the filling. If necessary, patch any gaps with more pastry, brushing them with oil.

7 Bake in a preheated oven, 200°C (400°F), Gas Mark 6, for 25–30 minutes until the pastry is golden and crisp.

8 To serve, sieve icing sugar over the top and make a random or lattice pattern with ground cinnamon, if liked.

Serves 6

1 small chicken

1 large onion, finely chopped

2 teaspoons grated fresh root ginger

good pinch of crushed saffron threads

3 tablespoons chopped fresh coriander

1½ teaspoons ground cinnamon

3 tablespoons chopped fresh parsley

4 eggs

25 g (1 oz) unsalted butter

75 g (3 oz) blanched almonds, chopped

2 teaspoons sugar

275 g (9 oz) packet filo pastry

olive oil, for brushing

salt and pepper

To serve:

icing sugar

ground cinnamon (optional)

chicken with almonds

Body is given to this simple, slightly spiced Moroccan sauce by finely chopped onion and almonds that are added at the beginning of the cooking so that they soften during the long, slow cooking.

1 Squeeze the lemon over the chicken, rub in the juice and season with salt and pepper. Mix together the ginger, cinnamon and saffron and spread over the chicken. Cover and leave at room temperature for about 1 hour.

2 Put the chicken quarters into a heavy flameproof casserole in which they just fit. Add the onion and almonds and sufficent water almost to cover. Bring just to simmering point, cover and simmer very gently for about 45–60 minutes, turning the chicken occasionally. Add the parsley and cook for a further 5 minutes.

3 Transfer the chicken to a warmed plate, cover and keep warm. Boil the cooking juices in the casserole to give a well-flavoured sauce, adjusting the levels of the spices and salt and pepper if necessary. Return the chicken to the casserole and turn in the sauce to coat completely.

Serves 4

1 lemon, halved

4 chicken quarters

½ teaspoon ground ginger

½ teaspoon ground cinnamon

pinch of saffron threads, toasted and crushed

1 Spanish onion, finely chopped

125 g (4 oz) blanched almonds, chopped

leaves from a large bunch of parsley, finely chopped

salt and pepper

chicken with coriander & lemon

I love this dish. It is clear-flavoured, simple and light, and the chicken is succulent and tender. What more could you ask?

1 Put the chicken breasts into a shallow glass or pottery bowl. Pour over the lemon rind and juice then add the cardamom, cumin, coriander and garlic. Cover and refrigerate for 24 hours, turning occasionally.

2 Heat the oil in a large, flameproof casserole. Add the onion and cook until translucent. Arrange the chicken on the chopped onion. Rinse the bowl with some of the stock and pour over the chicken. Add the remaining stock and the coriander and season with salt and pepper.

3 Heat to simmering point then cover the casserole and poach the chicken, turning it over twice, for about 40 minutes until the juices run clear when the thickest part is pierced with the point of a sharp knife.

4 Remove the chicken to a warmed serving platter. Boil the cooking juices if necessary to concentrate them, then serve with the chicken, accompanied by rice or bread.

Serves 4

4 chicken breasts

grated rind and juice of 1 lemon

seeds from 6 cardamom pods, roasted and crushed

1½ teaspoons ground cumin

1½ teaspoons ground coriander

1 garlic clove, crushed

2 tablespoons olive oil

1 onion, finely chopped

450 ml (¾ pint) chicken stock

bunch of coriander

salt and pepper

boiled rice or bread, to serve

chicken with olives & preserved lemons

2 tablespoons olive oil

1 Spanish onion, finely chopped

3 garlic cloves

1 teaspoon ground ginger

1½ teaspoons ground cinnamon

large pinch of saffron threads, toasted and crushed

1 chicken, weighing about 1.75 kg (3½ lb)

750 ml (1¼ pints) chicken stock or water

125 g (4 oz) pinky-brown Moroccan olives, rinsed, and soaked, if liked

1 preserved lemon (see right), rinsed if liked, chopped

large bunch of coriander, finely chopped

large bunch of parsley, finely chopped

salt and pepper

parsley leaves and coarsely chopped parsley, to garnish

This is one of the best-known Moroccan dishes. It cannot be made with fresh lemons, or, if it is, it will be an entirely different dish.

1   Heat the oil, add the onion and fry fairly gently, stirring frequenty until softened and a good golden colour.

2   Meanwhile, in a mortar, crush the garlic with a pinch of salt, then work in the ginger, cinnamon, saffron and a little pepper. Stir into the onions, cook until fragrant, then remove from the pan and spread over the chicken.

3   Put the chicken into a heavy saucepan or flameproof casserole that it just fits, add the stock or water and bring to just on simmering point. Cover and simmer very gently for about 1¼ hours, turning the chicken over 2–3 times.

4   Add the olives, preserved lemon, coriander and parsley to the pan, cover and cook for 15 minutes or so until the chicken is very tender. Taste the sauce – if the flavour needs to be more concentrated, transfer the chicken to a warmed serving dish, cover and keep warm, then boil the cooking juices to a rich sauce. Tilt the pan and skim off any surplus fat, if liked, then pour over the chicken and garnish with parsley.

Serves 4

preserved lemons

To preserve lemons: put 2 teaspoons coarse salt into a scalded Kilner jar. Holding a lemon over a plate to catch the juice, cut it lengthways as if about to quarter it, but do not cut quite through – leave the pieces joined. Ease out any pips. Pack 1 tablespoon salt into the cuts, then close them and place the lemon in the jar. Repeat with more lemons, packing them tightly, and pressing each layer down hard before adding the next layer, until the jar is full. Squeeze another lemon and pour the juice over the fruit. Sprinkle with more coarse salt and top up with boiling water to cover the lemons. Close the jar tightly and keep in a warmish place for 3–4 weeks. Do not worry if, on longer storage, a lacy white film appears on top of the jar or on the lemons; it is quite harmless – simply rinse it off.

lip-smacking chicken

Yet another very good example of the street finger food that I have enjoyed when visiting Morocco. To add a little fire to the dish, either spike the paste that is rubbed over the chicken with a little harissa (see page 80), or spread harissa sparingly over the chicken joints. Chicken breasts can also be used, and are very good served cold.

1 Crush the garlic with a pinch of salt then mix to a paste with the oil, coriander, cumin, paprika, parsley and lemon juice. Rub the spice mixture over the chicken then cover and leave in a cool place for 30 minutes to 2 hours.

2 Place the chicken on a preheated barbecue or about 10 cm (4 inches) below a preheated grill and cook for about 20 minutes, turning occasionally, until the juices run clear when the thickest part is tested with the point of a sharp knife. Scatter over coriander leaves and serve.

Serves 4

4 garlic cloves

4 tablespoons olive oil

1½ tablespoons ground coriander

1 tablespoon ground cumin

¾ teaspoon paprika

3 tablespoons chopped parsley

3 tablespoons lemon juice

8 large chicken drumsticks
or thighs

salt

coriander leaves, to garnish

honeyed chicken tagine

1 Heat the oil in a heavy flameproof casserole. Add the chicken and brown evenly. Remove to a plate.

2 Add the onion and garlic to the casserole and cook until softened but not browned.

3 Add the cinnamon and ginger and stir for 1 minute then return the chicken to the casserole. Add the lemon juice, honey and stock. Heat to just on simmering point then cover the casserole and cook gently for about 1 hour.

4 Transfer the chicken to a warmed platter, cover and keep warm. Add the raisins and almonds to the casserole and boil until the liquid is reduced and slightly syrupy. Season with salt and pepper, and lemon juice, if needed, to taste. Garnish with parsley and serve.

Serves 4

1 tablespoon olive oil

4 chicken portions

1 onion, chopped

2 garlic cloves, crushed

1 teaspoon ground cinnamon

½ teaspoon ground ginger

about 2 tablespoons lemon juice

2 tablepoons clear honey

250 ml (8 fl oz) chicken stock

50 g (2 oz) raisins

50 g (2 oz) flaked almonds

salt and pepper

parsley sprigs, to garnish

glazed spiced roast turkey

Turkey is always served for a meal of importance, a fine bird being a pleasure to the eye as well as to the taste buds. A honey glaze is typical, and gives a delicious, attractive crisp, golden brown skin.

1 Spread the almonds and sesame seeds on a baking sheet then put it in a preheated oven, 180°C (350°F), Gas Mark 4, for 8–10 minutes, stirring the mixture occasionally, until it is evenly browned. Set aside.

2 Meanwhile, mix together the cumin, coriander, cinnamon, ginger and ground cloves and season with salt and pepper. Rub the spice mixture over the skin of the turkey and in the cavity. Stick the whole cloves into the onion, put it in the cavity then sew up the opening with fine string.

3 Put the turkey on a rack in a roasting tin and spread the butter over the skin. Stir half of the stock into the honey. Cut the giblets into pieces and put them into the roasting tin with the cinnamon sticks. Pour the honey mixture over the bird then roast for 2½–3 hours until the juices run clear when the thickest part is pierced with a fine skewer. Turn the bird first on one side, then the other at regular intervals, and baste frequently with the honey/stock mixture. When it begins to brown, add the remaining stock.

4 About 30 minutes before the turkey is due to be served, remove it from the roasting tin. Strain the cooking juices into a heatproof jug. Skim off the fat. If there is more than about 250 ml (8 fl oz) glaze left in the jug, boil the juices to reduce them. Stir in the almond mixture.

5 Return the turkey to the roasting tin. Spread with the glaze then continue the cooking, basting frequently, until the skin is a rich golden brown and crisp.

6 Transfer the bird to a warmed carving dish, spoon over any remaining glaze, cover and leave in a warm place for 10–15 minutes before carving.

Serves 8–10

175 g (6 oz) blanched almonds, very finely chopped

2 tablespoons sesame seeds

1 tablespoon ground cumin

1 tablespoon ground coriander

2 tablespoons ground cinnamon

2 teaspoons ground ginger

1 teaspoon ground cloves

5 kg (10 lb) turkey, including giblets

5 whole cloves

1 onion, peeled

25 g (1 oz) butter, softened

500 ml (17 fl oz) chicken stock

125 ml (4 fl oz) clear honey

2 cinnamon sticks

salt and pepper

pigeon with kumquats

In countries where red meat can be limited, pigeons are a welcome addition to the diet. Every year, hundreds of birds pass over the Mediterranean on their journeys to and from their summer and winter haunts. Each time, many hapless birds, especially quail and pigeons, fall victim to the hunters' guns – to end up in the cooking pot. If kumquats are not available, add 2 peeled and thickly sliced oranges when the cooking liquid is almost reduced.

1 Heat the oil in a large, heavy flameproof casserole, add the pigeons in batches and cook until browned. Using a slotted spoon, transfer them to a dish. Stir the onions into the casserole and sauté until golden. Stir in the cinnamon, bay leaf, ginger, saffron, stock and salt and pepper and bring to the boil.

2 Return the pigeons to the casserole with any juices that have collected in the dish, cover and cook gently, turning the pigeons occasionally, for about 45 minutes, depending on their age, until they become tender.

3 Add the kumquats and honey, cover and cook for a further 30–45 minutes until the pigeons are very tender. Using a slotted spoon, transfer them to a large warmed serving platter, cover and keep warm.

4 Boil the cooking liquid until slightly thickened. Discard the cinnamon and bay leaf, if liked. Pour the liquid over the pigeons and scatter over the almonds.

Serves 6

3 tablespoons olive oil

6 young oven-ready pigeons

250 g (8 oz) button onions, peeled

1 cinnamon stick

1 bay leaf

¾–1 teaspoon grated fresh root ginger

large pinch of saffron threads, toasted and crushed

900 ml (1½ pints) chicken stock

250 g (8 oz) kumquats, halved

2 tablespoons clear honey

salt and pepper

lightly toasted almonds, to garnish

grains & pulses

Wheat is the staple grain. Not only is it made into the flour that is used for making the bread, and pastries, but the coarse grains of flour, or semolina, that are left after the finer grains have been removed are transformed into pellets of couscous (see page 7), which appears so frequently on Moroccan tables. That is not to say that rice is not served. It is, in both sweet and savoury dishes. Chickpeas are the favourite pulse; cooks will often go to the trouble of removing the outer skin to leave just the sweet, tender kernel inside. To do this, immerse the cooked chickpeas in a large bowl of cold water then gently rub handfuls of them between your fingers – the skins should slip off easily. Drop the chickpeas back in the water, where the skins will float to the surface. Drain the water and throw away the skins.

rice with tomatoes, avocado & black olives

4 tablespoons olive oil

1 small onion, finely chopped

2 plump garlic cloves, crushed

250 g (8 oz) basmati rice

450 ml (¾ pint) vegetable stock

1 well-flavoured tomato, deseeded and diced

2 spring onions, including some green, chopped

2 tablespoons chopped parsley

50 g (2 oz) black olives, pitted

1 small avocado, diced

salt and pepper

Serve this pretty mixture of white rice studded with vibrant green, pale green, black and red either hot or cold. It goes very well with seafood; here it has been served with fresh sardines and lemon wedges.

1 Heat 2 tablespoons of the oil in a saucepan. Add the onion and garlic and cook for 1 minute. Add the rice and stir for 2 minutes then add the stock and bring to the boil. Stir the rice then cover the pan and simmer very gently, without lifting the lid, for about 12 minutes until the rice is just tender.

2 Meanwhile, heat the remaining oil in a frying pan. Add the tomato, spring onions, parsley and salt and pepper and simmer for 5 minutes. Remove the pan from the heat and stir in the olives and avocado.

3 Fluff up the rice with a fork and carefully stir in the tomato mixture.

Serves 4

couscous, chickpea & prawn salad

This recipe started life as a hot dish with the couscous warmed over the chickpeas as they cooked. The prawns were added to the chickpeas during the latter stages of the cooking so the shellfish and pulse cooked together. This version is much easier. It would be a shame to miss it because it has an interesting combination of textures and tastes.

1 To make the dressing, whisk or shake together the oil and lemon juice. Add sugar, paprika, and salt and pepper taste.

2 Mix the couscous with the chickpeas, prawns, spring onions, tomatoes and mint. Pour over the dressing and toss to coat all the ingredients. Serve with lemon wedges.

Serves 4

175 g (6 oz) cooked couscous

400 g (13 oz) can chickpeas, drained and rinsed

500 g (1 lb) cooked peeled prawns

2 spring onions, thinly sliced

3 well-flavoured tomatoes, deseeded and chopped

bunch of mint, chopped

lemon wedges, to serve

Dressing:

6 tablespoons olive oil

3 tablespoons lemon juice

pinch of caster sugar

paprika

salt and pepper

green couscous

Couscous mixed with rocket, spring onions and cucumber makes an attractive accompaniment that harmonizes well with meat and fruit tagines. If you are unable to find rocket, substitute watercress.

1 Whisk or shake together the oil and lemon juice. Season to taste with salt and pepper.

2 Tip the couscous into a warmed serving dish. Stir in the spring onions, rocket, cucumber and oil and lemon juice dressing and serve straight away.

Serves 6

300 ml (½ pint) olive oil

125 ml (4 fl oz) lemon juice

500 g (1 lb) cooked couscous

2 bunches spring onions, chopped

125 g (4 oz) rocket, chopped

1 cucumber, halved, deseeded and chopped

salt and pepper

couscous & pepper pilaff

1 Heat the oil in a saucepan, add the onion and cook until it begins to soften. Stir in the garlic, chilli and peppers. Cook for 3–4 minutes then season with paprika and cook for 1 minute.

2 Add the couscous, give it a good stir, then add the boiling stock. Bring to the boil then simmer gently, uncovered, for about 15 minutes until most of the stock has been absorbed and the peppers are tender; if the pilaff becomes too dry add a little more stock or water.

3 To serve, add salt to taste and stir in the coriander.

Serves 2 as a light supper or 4 as a side dish

3 tablespoons olive oil

1 red onion or small onion, finely chopped

2 plump garlic cloves, crushed

1 fresh red chilli, deseeded and finely chopped

1 red pepper, cored, deseeded and cut lengthways into 8 pieces

1 yellow pepper, cored, deseeded and cut lengthways into 8 pieces

paprika

250 g (8 oz) couscous

300 ml (½ pint) boiling vegetable stock

small handful of coriander leaves, chopped

salt

pumpkin & couscous pilaff

1 Put the couscous into a bowl. Pour over the water and leave to soak for 15 minutes. Add the saffron to the stock and set aside to soak.

2 Heat 3 tablespoons of the oil in a saucepan. Add the onion and fry until translucent, then add the pumpkin and fry until the onion and pumpkin are lightly coloured.

3 Drain the couscous and add to the pan with the saffron liquid, lemon rind, cinnamon, bay leaves and salt and pepper. Bring to the boil then simmer very gently, uncovered, until most of the liquid has evaporated.

4 Meanwhile, heat the remaining oil in a heavy frying pan, add the almonds and cook, stirring frequently, until evenly browned.

5 Remove the cinnamon, bay leaves and lemon rind from the pilaff, if liked, then fork in the almonds. Garnish with mint or dill and serve.

Serves 4

150 g (5 oz) couscous

200 ml (7 fl oz) water

½ teaspoon saffron threads

250 ml (8 fl oz) vegetable stock

4 tablespoons olive oil

1 onion, finely chopped

400 g (13 oz) pumpkin, diced

long strip of lemon rind

1 cinnamon stick

2 bay leaves

125 g (4 oz) flaked almonds

salt and pepper

sprigs of mint or dill, to garnish

aubergines with fruited couscous

Grilled sliced aubergines are served over fragrant couscous studded with fresh fruits, making a wonderful dish in its own right or a splendid accompaniment to roast or grilled meats or poultry.

1 Sprinkle the aubergine slices with salt and leave to drain for about 1 hour. Rinse thoroughly and dry well.

2 Meanwhile, heat the oil, add the mixed spice, cinnamon, coriander and cumin and stir for about 1 minute. Add the pine nuts and sugar, stir for 1 further minute then add the raisins, dates, physalis, stock, coriander and lemon juice. Bring to the boil. Stir in the couscous, cover the pan and remove from the heat. Leave to stand, stirring every 3 minutes, until the grains swell. (It will stay warm for 30 minutes.)

3 To make the sauce, heat the oil, add the onion and cook until softened and lightly coloured, adding the garlic when the onion is almost done. Add the mixed spice and cinnamon and stir for 1 minute. Add the stock and apricots and simmer gently for 20 minutes.

4 Brush the aubergine slices with oil and grill until tender and browned, then season them with salt and pepper.

5 To serve, season the couscous with salt and pepper and pile on to a warmed platter, pour over some of the sauce, arrange the aubergine slices on top and garnish with mint sprigs. Serve the remaining sauce separately.

Serves 4

2 aubergines, cut lengthways into 1 cm (½ inch) slices

4 tablespoons olive oil, plus extra for brushing

1 tablespoon mixed spice

1 teaspoon ground cinnamon

1 teaspoon ground coriander

1 teaspoon ground cumin

2 tablespoons pine nuts

1 tablespoon soft brown sugar

50 g (2 oz) raisins

50 g (2 oz) pitted fresh dates, coarsely chopped

100 g (3½ oz) physalis (Cape gooseberries), halved

450 ml (¾ pint) vegetable or chicken stock

2 tablespoons chopped fresh coriander

1 tablespoon lemon juice

275 g (9 oz) couscous

salt and pepper

mint sprigs, to garnish

Sauce:

2 tablespoons olive oil

1 small onion, finely chopped

1 garlic clove, crushed

1 tablespoon mixed spice

1 teaspoon ground cinnamon

300 ml (½ pint) vegetable stock

50 g (2 oz) ready-to-eat dried apricots, chopped

nutty couscous & rice salad

1 Put the couscous into a bowl and pour over the boiling water. Leave to soak for about 15 minutes until the water has been absorbed, fluffing up the couscous with a fork occasionally.

2 Meanwhile, cook the rice in a large saucepan of boiling salted water for 12–15 minutes until tender.

3 To make the dressing, whisk or shake together the oil, lemon juice and vinegar then season to taste.

4 Heat the oil in a frying pan. Add the chilli, garlic, almonds and pine nuts. Cook, stirring occasionally, until the nuts have browned.

5 Drain the rice and transfer to a warmed serving bowl. Fluff it up with a fork then toss in the couscous, the nut mixture, apricots, raisins, mint and parsley and the dressing.

Serves 4

250 g (8 oz) couscous

450 ml (¾ pint) boiling water

175 g (6 oz) white long-grain rice

2 tablespoons olive oil

1 fresh red chilli, deseeded and finely chopped

1 plump garlic clove, crushed

125 g (4 oz) blanched almonds, coarsely chopped

4 tablespoons pine nuts

125 g (4 oz) ready-to-eat dried apricots, coarsely chopped

25 g (1 oz) plump raisins

6 tablespoons mixed chopped mint and parsley

Dressing:

150 ml (5 fl oz) olive oil

4 tablespoons mixed lemon juice and white wine vinegar

salt and pepper

chickpeas with tomatoes & spinach

1 Put the aubergines into a colander, sprinkle with salt and leave to drain for 1 hour then rinse them well and dry thoroughly.

2 Heat the oil in a large frying pan. Add the aubergines in batches and cook until browned on the outside and tender inside. Remove with a slotted spoon and drain on kitchen paper.

3 If necessary, add a little extra oil to the pan. When it is hot, add the onion and fry until soft and golden, adding the garlic, ginger and chilli when it is almost done. Stir in the cumin and coriander for 30 seconds then return the aubergines and add the chickpeas, the tomatoes and their juice and the water. Simmer gently for 15 minutes.

4 Add the spinach, and more water if necessary, bring to the boil and cook for 1–2 minutes until the spinach wilts. Season to taste and serve.

Serves 4

3 aubergines, cut into 2.5 cm (1 inch) pieces

about 4 tablespoons olive oil

1 onion, chopped

4 garlic cloves, crushed

1 cm (½ inch) piece of fresh root ginger, peeled and grated

1 fresh red chilli, deseeded and chopped

2 teaspoons ground cumin

2 teaspoons ground coriander

2 x 400 g (13 oz) cans chickpeas, drained and rinsed

2 x 400 g (13 oz) cans chopped tomatoes

125 ml (4 fl oz) water

500 g (1 lb) small spinach leaves

salt and pepper

bean tagine

1 Boil the beans in unsalted water for 10 minutes then drain. Tie the celery, bay leaves and parsley together with kitchen string. Cover the beans with fresh unsalted water, add the celery and herbs and simmer for about 1 hour until the beans are just tender. Drain, reserving the cooking liquid, and discard the celery and herbs.

2 Meanwhile, make the sauce. Empty the tomatoes and their juice into a saucepan, add the oil, parsley and sugar and bring to the boil then simmer, uncovered, for about 20 minutes until thick.

3 Heat the oil in a heavy flameproof casserole. Add the onion, garlic, chillies, red peppers and paprika and cook gently for 5 minutes. Stir in the beans, the sauce and enough of the reserved cooking liquid to just cover the beans. Season with salt and pepper, cover and cook in a preheated oven, 150°C (300°F), Gas Mark 2, for 1½ hours, stirring occasionally.

4 Just before serving, stir in the mint, parsley and coriander. Garnish with mint leaves and serve with a bowl of Harissa, if you like.

Serves 8

500 g (1 lb) red or white kidney beans, soaked overnight and drained

2 celery sticks, halved

2 bay leaves

4 parsley sprigs

4 tablespoons olive oil

500 g (1 lb) onions, chopped

5 garlic cloves, crushed

2 fresh red chillies, deseeded and chopped

4 red peppers, cored, deseeded and chopped

1 tablespoon paprika

large handful of mixed chopped mint, parsley and coriander

salt and pepper

mint leaves, to garnish

Harissa (see page 80), to serve (optional)

Sauce:

900 g (2 lb) can chopped tomatoes

2 tablespoons olive oil

4 parsley sprigs

1 tablespoon sugar

2 aubergines, cut into 5 cm (2 inch) chunks

2 courgettes, cut into 5 cm (2 inch) chunks

1 red pepper, cored, deseeded and cut lengthways into 6 pieces

1 yellow pepper, cored, deseeded and cut lenthways into 6 pieces

1 fennel bulb, root end left on, cut into 6 wedges

3 red onions, root ends left on, each cut into 6 wedges

4 tablespoons olive oil

3 garlic cloves, crushed

Tabasco sauce

750 ml (1¼ pints) vegetable stock

500 g (1 lb) couscous

1 onion, finely diced

salt and pepper

couscous with roast vegetables

1 Put the aubergines, cougettes, red and yellow peppers, fennel and red onions into a roasting tin. Add 3 tablespoons of the olive oil, 2 of the garlic cloves, 2 or 3 dashes of Tabasco sauce and pepper. Stir all the ingredients, then roast for about 35 minutes in a preheated oven on its highest setting until the vegetables are charred and tender.

2 Meanwhile, bring the stock to the boil in a saucepan, add the couscous, stir, then cover the pan and remove from the heat. Leave to stand until the stock has been absorbed.

3 Heat the remaining oil in a frying pan, add the onion and fry until tender and golden, adding the remaining garlic towards the end. Stir the onion mixture into the couscous and season to taste with salt and pepper.

4 Serve the roast vegetables piled on to the couscous.

Serves 6

fragrant rice

Traditional recipes usually specify soaking the rice, but while this may have been necessary at one time, with the rice now available I find it makes no difference to the finished dish. Washing, however, is still essential, as it removes surplus surface starch. Saffron will bring joy and happiness – or so folklore decrees – but even if it falls short on this count, it will definitely add a sunny colour and its own inimitable flavour and aroma.

250 g (8 oz) basmati rice

seeds from 4 cardamom pods, crushed

large pinch of saffron threads, crushed (optional)

1 cinnamon stick

1½ teaspoons cumin seeds

2 bay leaves

1 tablespoon olive oil

1 onion, chopped

600 ml (1 pint) water

2 tablespoons lemon juice

75 g (3 oz) raisins (optional)

50 g (2 oz) pine nuts, browned in oil

salt and pepper

1 Wash the rice until the water runs clear. Put the cardamom seeds, saffron, cinnamon, cumin seeds and bay leaves in a large, heavy flameproof casserole and dry-fry over a moderate heat for 2–3 minutes until fragrant. Add the oil and, when it is hot, stir in the onion and cook gently for about 10 minutes, stirring frequently, until it has softened and lightly browned.

2 Add the rice, turning to coat the grains in the oil. Stir in the water, lemon juice, raisins, if using, and salt and pepper. Bring to the boil, cover and simmer for 15 minutes without lifting the lid, until the rice is just tender, all the water has been absorbed and small holes puncture the surface. Remove from the heat and leave, covered, for a few minutes. Fork through the pine nuts and serve.

Serves 4

2 tablespoons olive oil

1 Spanish onion, chopped

4 garlic cloves, crushed

4 carrots, chopped

1 teaspoon ground coriander

1 teaspoon ground cumin

1 teaspoon ground cinnamon

175 g (6 oz) pearl barley

1.2 litres (2 pints) vegetable stock

2 courgettes, chopped

500 g (1 lb) cooked chickpeas

50 g (2 oz) plump raisins

125 g (4 oz) flaked almonds

bunch of parsley, chopped

salt and pepper

barley & chickpea pilaff

Barley and chickpeas make an interesting combination of textures and flavours, which is enhanced by the spices, raisins and almonds in this recipe.

1 Heat the oil in a saucepan. Add the onion, garlic and carrots and cook for 5 minutes. Add the coriander, cumin and cinnamon and stir for 1 minute then stir in the barley. When the spices are thoroughly mixed, add the stock. Bring to the boil, cover the pan and simmer gently for 15 minutes.

2 Add the courgettes to the pan, cover and simmer gently for 10 minutes.

3 Add the chickpeas, raisins, almonds and parsley and mix into the vegetables. Season with salt and pepper and cook for 5 minutes.

Serves 6

rice & lentil pilaff

One-pot dishes are a feature of the traditional cooking of Morocco, Algeria and Tunisia, where it makes sense to use the minimum number of cooking pots. It's a practice I fully agree with, especially when it produces such tasty dishes as this one.

1 Layer the aubergine in a colander, sprinkling salt between the layers. Leave for at least 1 hour then rinse well and dry thoroughly.

2 Heat the oil in a large heavy-based saucepan. Add the onion, garlic, carrots and aubergine and fry for 5 minutes, stirring occasionally.

3 Stir the ginger, paprika, coriander and cumin into the pan and cook, stirring, for 1 minute then stir in the lentils and rice. When well mixed, add the stock. Bring to the boil, cover the pan and simmer gently, stirring occasionally, for 30–35 minutes until the rice and lentils are tender and the stock has been absorbed.

4 Stir in the spinach and cook for 2 minutes until it has thoroughly wilted. Season to taste with salt and pepper and scatter with the sesame seeds.

Serves 4

1 small aubergine, weighing about 250 g (8 oz), cut into cubes

2 tablespoons olive oil

1 onion, finely chopped

4 garlic cloves, crushed

2 carrots, chopped

1 teaspoon ground ginger

1 teaspoon paprika

1 teaspoon ground coriander

1 teaspoon ground cumin

250 g (8 oz) red lentils

250 g (8 oz) white long-grain rice

1 litre (1¾ pints) vegetable stock

250 g (8 oz) spinach, shredded

2 tablespoons sesame seeds, lightly toasted

salt and pepper

vegetables & salads

Morocco provides a remarkable range of vegetables. You will find tender turnips, glowing baby aubergines, vibrant red peppers, the most flavourful tomatoes you can imagine, delicate broad beans, artichokes, both globe and Jerusalem, celery and cauliflower and of course heads of garlic by the dozen. All these, and more, will be displayed with pride on the stalls in the souks and by the road in the countryside. Looking so fresh and in prime condition, these vegetables beg to be bought. Having been prepared with skill, when they are in the cooking pot they yield their flavour readily to all manner of dishes. They also provide a myriad of different textures.

honey-glazed turnips

Moroccan turnips are beautifully tender with a delicious, gentle and sweet flavour. Both of these qualities are highlighted by the simple treatment in this recipe.

750 g (1½ lb) baby turnips

50 g (2 oz) unsalted butter

2 heaped tablespoons clear honey

2 tablespoons toasted flaked almonds

1½ tablespoons chopped fresh coriander

salt and pepper

1 Cook the turnips in boiling salted water for about 10 minutes until tender but still firm to the bite. Drain.

2 Melt the butter with the honey in a frying pan. Add the turnips and cook, stirring, for 3–5 minutes until glossy.

3 Stir in the almonds then pile the turnips into a warmed serving dish. Season with salt and pepper. Pour over the pan juices and sprinkle with the coriander.

Serves 4–6

potatoes with harissa, peppers & tomatoes

3 tablespoons olive oil

750 g (1½ lb) potatoes, cut into chunks

1 large onion, sliced

2 red peppers, cored, deseeded and sliced

1 yellow pepper, cored, deseeded and sliced

4 well-flavoured tomatoes, cut into chunks

3 garlic cloves, crushed

3–4 teaspoons Harissa (see page 80)

salt

1 Heat 1 tablespoon of the oil in a large frying pan. Add the potatoes, stir to coat them in the oil, then cover the pan and fry over a low heat for 15 minutes, shaking the pan occasionally.

2 Add the remaining oil to the pan, then add the onion and red and yellow peppers. Increase the heat and cook, uncovered, for 10 minutes, stirring frequently, until the peppers have browned.

3 Add the tomatoes and garlic and continue to cook for about 4 minutes until the tomatoes have softened. Add the harissa, season with salt and serve.

Serves 4

fried spinach with nuts

This salad is usually made with bokkola, or mallow. It grows wild in the country, where it can be picked for free. It is not an uncommon sight in North Africa to see children selling large bunches of mallow by the roadside.

1 Heat half of the olive oil in a large sauté pan or deep frying pan. Add the pine nuts or almonds and fry, stirring frequently, until lightly browned. Using a slotted spoon, transfer the nuts to kitchen paper to drain.

2 Add half of the onion and garlic to the pan and fry until beginning to soften. Add half of the spinach and cook over a high heat for 4–5 minutes until the leaves have wilted and most of the liquid has evaporated. Transfer the spinach mixture to a warmed colander.

3 Add the remaining oil to the pan. When it has heated, cook the remaining onion, garlic and spinach. Transfer the first batch of spinach from the colander to a warmed serving dish before adding the second batch to the colander.

4 Meanwhile, whisk or shake together the virgin olive oil, orange juice and rind. Season with freshly grated nutmeg, salt and pepper.

5 Add the remaining spinach to the serving dish and mix with the dressing. Scatter with the nuts and serve.

Serves 4

4 tablespoons olive oil

50 g (2 oz) pine nuts or flaked almonds

1 large onion, finely chopped

2 garlic cloves, crushed

1 kg (2 lb) small spinach leaves

1 tablespoon virgin olive oil

juice of 1 orange

grated rind of ½ orange

freshly grated nutmeg

salt and pepper

stuffed aubergines

By the same token that older British cooks would not recognise much of today's so-called British cooking, older Moroccan cooks may not appreciate that this dish hails from a Moroccan kitchen, but it does. The aubergines can be served as a side dish to grilled meats or poultry, or as a first course or light lunch or supper.

1 Score the cut flesh of the aubergines deeply, taking care not to pierce the skins. Brush with the oil then put them, cut-side up, on a baking sheet and cook in a preheated oven, 200°C (400°F), Gas Mark 6, for 20–30 minutes until the flesh is soft.

2 Meanwhile, put the couscous into a heatproof bowl, pour over the boiling water and leave to soak for 10–15 minutes.

3 To make the sauce, mix together all the ingredients, except the garnish, in a bowl. Cover and chill.

4 Scoop the flesh from the aubergines and chop finely. Using a fork, mix the aubergine flesh with the couscous, adding the dried apricots, spring onions, tomato, mint and pine nuts at the same time. Add the lemon juice and season to taste with salt and pepper.

5 Pile the couscous mixture into the aubergines and return to the oven for about 15 minutes to heat through. Garnish the sauce with a coriander sprig and serve with the aubergines.

Serves 4

2 aubergines, about 275 g (9 oz) each, halved lengthways

olive oil, for brushing

50 g (2 oz) couscous

150 ml (¼ pint) boiling water

25 g (1 oz) ready-to-eat dried apricots, chopped

4 spring onions, chopped

1 large, well-flavoured tomato, deseeded and chopped

leaves from 8 mint sprigs, chopped

1 tablespoon pine nuts, chopped

1 tablespoon lemon juice

salt and pepper

Sauce:

1 garlic clove, crushed

grated rind and juice of 1 lime

1 cm (½ inch) piece of fresh root ginger, peeled and grated

2 tablespoons chopped fresh coriander

150 ml (¼ pint) Greek yogurt

coriander sprig, to garnish

baked aubergines with red peppers & almonds

Served either hot or cold, this dish can accompany roast or grilled meats, poultry or fish. I have also eaten it as part of a first course spread.

1 Put the aubergine slices on a baking sheet. Brush generously with oil and sprinkle over thyme and black pepper. Add the red pepper quarters to the baking sheet.

2 Bake the vegetables in a preheated oven, 200°C (400°F), Gas Mark 6, for 10 minutes. Toss the nuts in olive oil and add to the baking sheet. Bake for a further 5–10 minutes until the aubergines are tender.

3 Transfer the vegetables and nuts to a serving dish and sprinkle mint leaves and more black pepper over the top. Serve warm or leave in a cold place, not the refrigerator, overnight to allow the flavours to develop.

Serves 2–4

2 aubergines, cut into 1 cm (½ inch) slices

olive oil

thyme leaves, for sprinkling

2 red peppers, cored, deseeded and quartered

2 tablespoons flaked almonds or pine nuts

pepper

torn mint leaves, to garnish

vegetable tagine

Just as almost any vegetable can be used in a vegetable stew or casserole, so they can in a tagine. Some combinations are more successful than others. This is a good one.

1 Heat the oil in a saucepan. Add the onion, garlic, celery and carrots and cook until beginning to brown. Add the harissa and stir for 1 minute.

2 Add the aubergines, tomatoes and the water to the pan. Bring to the boil then cover the pan and simmer gently for about 25 minutes.

3 Stir the okra into the pan, cover and cook for 15–20 minutes until the okra is tender.

4 If necessary, uncover the pan towards the end of cooking so the consistency of the sauce at the end of the cooking is quite thick. Add salt to taste. Serve garnished with chopped coriander.

Serves 4

1 tablespoon virgin olive oil

1 red onion, cut into wedges

2 garlic cloves, crushed

3 celery sticks, sliced

3 carrots, thinly sliced

2 teaspoons Harissa (see page 80)

about 625 g (1¼ lb) small aubergines, chopped

2 large well-flavoured tomatoes, chopped

250 ml (8 fl oz) water

125 g (4 oz) small okra, trimmed

salt

chopped fresh coriander, to garnish

sweet potato & pea tagine

I have subdued the original flavourings of this Tunisian recipe so that the combination of lemon juice, honey, cinnamon and chillies subtley complements the flavour of sweet potatoes, but if you prefer a dish with a punchier flavour, increase the quantities.

1 Mix together 1 tablespoon of the lemon juice and all of the honey, cinnamon and chilli powder. Set aside.

2 Heat the oil in a large, heavy frying pan, add the sweet potatoes and cook, stirring occasionally, for 10 minutes. Add the onion, garlic, salt, the remaining lemon juice and the water. Cook, stirring occasionally, for about 5 minutes until the onion begins to brown. Add the spiced honey mixture and cook, stirring, for 2 minutes, then serve.

Serves 4

4 tablespoons lemon juice

3–4 teaspoons clear honey

1 teaspoon ground cinnamon

¼ teaspoon chilli powder, or to taste

2 tablespoons olive oil

750 g (1½ lb) sweet potatoes, cut into 1 cm (½ inch) cubes

1 onion, finely chopped

2 garlic cloves, finely chopped

4 tablespoons water

salt

carrot salad with cinnamon, lemon & honey

I have lost track of the different North African versions of carrot salad that I have been served and have made and eaten, yet alone the innumerable recipes that I have seen in books and magazines. Some of the salads use cooked carrots while others call for raw carrots, either sliced or grated. Sweetness is a common feature. Flavourings include orange juice and rind, orange flower water and rosewater and the characteristic Moroccan spices such as cinnamon, ginger, cardamom and cumin. Plump raisins or dried apricots often make an appearance, as do almonds. This is my current favourite.

500 g (1 lb) young carrots, grated

50 g (2 oz) plump raisins

75 ml (3 fl oz) virgin olive oil

juice of 1 lemon

1 teaspoon ground cinnamon

1 tablespoon clear honey

salt and pepper

lightly toasted flaked almonds, to garnish

1 Put the carrots and raisins into a serving bowl.

2 Whisk or shake together the oil, lemon juice, cinnamon and honey. Season to taste with salt and pepper then pour the dressing over the carrots and raisins and toss to mix.

3 Scatter with the almonds and serve.

Serves 4

radish salad

Radishes have the type of hot peppery flavour that is so loved in Morocco. The crisp vegetables are nibbled, just as they come, as a palate cleanser before a meal or after a rich dish. Sliced radishes are often combined with oranges in an excellent combination that is eaten as part of a first course spread. I also like to serve it to counterbalance a rich or heavy main course, either with it or afterwards.

2–3 bunches of radishes, trimmed and thinly sliced

2 oranges, peeled and segmented

2–3 tablespoons lemon juice

caster sugar, to taste

orange flower water (optional)

salt

ground cinnamon or chopped coriander, to serve

1 Toss together the radishes and oranges.

2 Mix the lemon juice with sugar, orange flower water if using, and salt to taste, stirring until the sugar and salt have dissolved. Pour over the salad and toss lightly.

3 Serve the salad straight away sprinkled with a fine dusting of cinnamon, or chopped coriander.

Serves 4–6

roast vegetable salad

The use of charcoal grills is not confined to meat and fish; they also work wonders with vegetables, concentrating their flavours and bringing out the natural sweetness. If possible, make the salad a day in advance and keep it, covered, in a cool place but not the refrigerator. This salad is traditionally served as part of a selection of dishes for a first course, but it could be served as a main course, especially with boiled eggs, pickled lemons and perhaps tuna.

1 Put the aubergines in a roasting tin and roast in a preheated oven, 220°C (425°F), Gas Mark 7, for 20 minutes.

2 Add the peppers, garlic and tomatoes and 2 tablespoons of the oil and return to the oven for 20 minutes. Remove the vegetables from the oven and leave them until they are cool enough to handle.

3 Peel and coarsely chop the aubergines, and peel and slice the peppers; leave the garlic whole (the roast cloves are delicious mashed with the juices when you eat the salad).

4 Put the vegetables back in the roasting tin, stir in the chilli, caraway seeds, lemon juice and olives. Season with a little salt then cook, uncovered, for 10–15 minutes until the liquid has evaporated.

5 Remove the salad from the oven and leave to cool. Transfer the salad to a serving dish and scatter with the mint. Serve at room temperature.

Serves 6

500 g (1 lb) aubergines

4 red peppers, halved, cored and deseeded

6 garlic cloves, unpeeled

6 tomatoes

4 tablespoons olive oil

1 fresh red chilli, deseeded and finely chopped

½ teaspoon caraway seeds

2 tablespoons lemon juice

small handful of black olives, pitted

salt

2 tablespoons chopped mint, to garnish

grilled red pepper & tomato salad

3 large red peppers

4 well-flavoured tomatoes

4 whole garlic cloves, unpeeled

2 tablespoons virgin olive oil

small handful of chopped parsley and coriander, to serve (optional)

salt and pepper

1 Cook the peppers, tomatoes and garlic under a preheated grill, turning occasionally, until the skins of the peppers and tomatoes are evenly charred and blistered and the garlic cloves are soft.

2 When they are cool enough to handle, peel the peppers and tomatoes, cut them into quarters and remove the cores and seeds. Arrange on a serving plate.

3 Peel the garlic then mash into the oil. Season with salt and pepper and spoon over the peppers and tomatoes. Leave to marinate overnight in a cool place, not the refrigerator. Scatter over the herbs, if using, just before serving.

Serves 4

minted cucumber and tomato salad

½ large cucumber, peeled and halved lengthways

4 well-flavoured tomatoes, sliced

2 spring onions, finely chopped

1 tablespoon lemon juice

2 tablespoons extra virgin olive oil

pinch of sugar

2 tablespoons chopped mint leaves

1 teaspoon finely chopped Preserved Lemon rind (see page 102)

salt and pepper

The fresh flavours of mint and lemon perk up a plain cucumber and tomato salad, making it ideal as part of a first course spread or as an accompaniment to grilled or roast meats.

1 Scoop out the seeds from the cucumber. Slice the cucumber and arrange it on a serving plate with the sliced tomato. Sprinkle over the spring onions.

2 Whisk together the lemon juice and oil and season with sugar and salt. Pour the dressing over the salad.

3 Scatter the mint leaves and lemon rind over the salad and grind over black pepper. Cover and chill lightly before serving.

Serves 4

warm chickpea salad

Chickpeas are the firmest, nuttiest-tasting dried bean so they make good salads. But it is best to warm them in the dressing (because they are firm there is no danger of them disintegrating) so they absorb the other flavours.

1 Heat 1 tablespoon of the oil in a frying pan, add the onion, garlic and ginger and cook gently for 5–7 minutes until soft and transparent.

2 Add the chickpeas, chilli flakes and lemon rind and stir for about 30 seconds, then add the lemon juice and let the mixture bubble until it is almost dry. Add the coriander and season to taste with salt and pepper.

3 Turn the chickpea mixture into a warm serving bowl and pour over the remaining oil. Sprinkle a little ground cumin and paprika over the top.

Serves 4

5 tablespoons virgin olive oil

1 red onion, finely chopped

2 garlic cloves, finely crushed

4 cm (1½ inch) piece of fresh root ginger, grated

2 x 400 g (13 oz) cans chickpeas, drained

pinch of dried chilli flakes

juice and finely grated rind of 1½ lemons

leaves from a bunch of coriander, chopped

salt and pepper

mixed ground cumin and paprika, to serve

vegetable kebabs

1 Layer the aubergine cubes in a colander, sprinkling salt between the layers. Leave for at least 1 hour. Rinse well and dry thoroughly.

2 Meanwhile, crush the cardamom seeds with 1 of the garlic cloves and a pinch of salt in a large bowl, then mix with the turmeric and lemon juice. Whisk in 4 tablespoons of the oil and add pepper to taste. Stir in the spring onion and the aubergine cubes and cover them evenly in the spiced oil.

3 Crush the remaining garlic with 2 bay leaves and a pinch of salt. Mix in the remaining oil and the coriander. Season with pepper. Stir in the red peppers and onions so that they are well coated with the oil. Leave in a cool place for at least 1 hour.

4 Thread the aubergines, peppers and onions alternately on to metal skewers, with the whole bay leaves.

5 Cook the kebabs on a hot barbecue or under a preheated grill, turning them occasionally, for 8–10 minutes until the vegetables are tender and browned.

Serves 4

2 aubergines, cut into 2.5 cm (1 inch) cubes

seeds from 12 cardamom pods

2 garlic cloves

½ teaspoon ground turmeric

juice of ½ lemon

6 tablespoons olive oil

1 spring onion, finely chopped

14 bay leaves

2 tablespoons chopped fresh coriander

2 red peppers, cored, deseeded and cut into chunks

2 large red onions, quartered then halved

salt and pepper

orange & olive salad

You need to apply the opposite criteria to normal when choosing the oranges for this salad because the ones that work best have a sharp flavour, not a sweet taste. The olives should be large and fleshy.

1 Heat a small heavy frying pan, add the cumin seeds and dry-fry until fragrant. Tip into a grinder and grind to a powder.

2 Remove the rind from 1 of the oranges with a zester and set aside. Peel the oranges with a sharp knife, carefully removing all the pith. Working over a bowl to catch the juice, cut out the segments from the oranges and discard any pips. Put the oranges and olives into the bowl.

3 Whisk or shake together the oil, harissa and roast cumin. Add salt to taste then pour the dressing over the oranges and olives and toss together.

4 Arrange the lettuce leaves in a serving bowl. Add the orange and olive mixture. Garnish with the reserved orange rind and dill sprigs and serve.

Serves 4

2 teaspoons cumin seeds

4 large oranges

125 g (4 oz) green olives

50 ml (2 fl oz) virgin olive oil

1 tablespoon Harissa (see page 80), or to taste

1 crisp lettuce, torn into bite-size pieces

salt

dill sprigs, to garnish

pastries, desserts & teas

Meals usually end with fresh fruit, which is luscious, plentiful and cheap, although occasionally there will be a pudding such as Rice Pudding (see page 141) or Rosewater Pudding (see page 140). Pastries, which are notoriously sweet and rich, are normally eaten with glasses of tea at any time of the day, and are offered to guests. They are also served by the trayful at special occasions such as festivals and family celebrations. The majority of these pastries are usually bought rather than made at home.

gazelle's horns

200 g (7 oz) plain flour, plus extra for dusting

2 tablespoons sunflower oil

150–175ml (5–6 fl oz) mixed orange flower water and water

icing sugar, for dusting

Filling:

200 g (7 oz) blanched almonds, ground

100 g (3½ oz) caster sugar

½ teaspoon ground cinnamon

about 2 tablespoons orange flower water

These popular curved, horn-shaped pastries are often known by their French name, cornet de gazelles, *and various versions are met not only in Morocco but right across North Africa.*

1 To make the filling, mix all the ingredients together then knead to a paste; it will seem dry at first but as the warmth of your hands releases the oil in the almonds the mixture will soften and stick together. Set aside.

2 Sift the flour into a bowl. Mix in the oil and just enough orange flower water and water to make a soft dough. Knead until smooth and elastic.

3 On a lightly floured surface, roll out the dough very thinly and cut it into 7.5 cm (3 inch) wide strips. Roll pieces of filling about the size of a walnut into thin sausage shapes approximately 7.5 cm (3 inches) long and with tapering ends. Place lengthways along the edge of the strips of dough, about 3 cm (1¼ inches) apart.

4 Dampen the edges of the dough with water and fold over to enclose the filling. Press the edges together to seal. Use a pastry cutter to cut around the humps of filling. Press the cut edges together to seal.

5 Carefully curve the pastries into crescent or horn shapes and place on a baking sheet. Bake in a preheated oven, 180°C (350°F), Gas Mark 4, for 20–25 minutes until lightly coloured. Transfer to a wire rack to cool. Dust with icing sugar before serving.

Makes about 16

almond biscuits

2 small eggs

200 g (7 oz) icing sugar, plus extra
for coating

2 teaspoons baking powder

400 g (13 oz) ground almonds

grated rind of ½ lemon

orange flower water or rosewater,
to taste

oil

Rich and with a crazed appearance, these biscuits (pictured on page 139) are a popular sweetmeat. They are delicious served with coffee, or creamy or fruity desserts. You may find that the mixture becomes too sticky to handle, depending on the warmth of your hands and the kitchen; if this does happen, pop the mixture in the refrigerator to firm up.

1 Break 1 whole egg and 1 egg yolk into a bowl then beat in the sugar and baking powder until thoroughly combined. Work in the ground almonds, lemon rind and orange flower water or rosewater to taste. Knead well so the warmth of your hands releases the oil in the almonds to make a soft, workable paste; if necessary, add the extra egg white.

2 With oiled hands, roll walnut-size pieces of the mixture into egg-shaped balls. Cover a plate with icing sugar. Flatten the balls on the plate, covering them in the sugar.

3 Place the almond balls, spaced well apart, on an oiled baking sheet and bake in a preheated oven, 180°C (350°F), Gas Mark 4, for about 15 minutes until golden. Transfer to a wire rack to cool. Store in an airtight container.

Makes about 30

rosewater pudding

5 tablespoons cornflour

3–5 tablespoons sugar, to taste

750 ml (1¼ pints) creamy milk

2 tablespoons rosewater

½ teaspoon grated lemon rind
(optional)

50 g (2 oz) mixed blanched
almonds and pistachios, chopped

The texture of this delightful pudding is very reminiscent of nursery food – light, silky, soothing and not quite set. The 'new' flavouring of rosewater turns it into an adult dessert.

1 Blend the cornflour, a little sugar and a few spoonfuls of the milk to a paste. Bring the remaining milk to the boil in a saucepan, preferably a non-stick one, then stir some into the paste. Return to the saucepan and cook, stirring, until thick enough to coat the back of the spoon.

2 Remove the pan from the heat and stir in the rosewater and lemon rind if using. Add more sugar if needed. Pour into a large serving dish, or individual dishes, and leave until a skin forms on the surface.

3 Scatter the nuts over the top of the pudding(s), then leave until cold. Cover and chill before serving.

Serves 4–6

almond pastry snake

1 Stir the ground almonds and icing sugar together and mix to a paste with the egg white, almond essence and rosewater. Divide into 3 equal pieces. Sift icing sugar over the work surface then roll out each piece of almond paste to a 47.5 cm (19 inch) long 'sausage', about 1 cm (½ inch) thick.

2 Brush a sheet of filo pastry with oil, cover with a second sheet of pastry and brush that with oil; cover the unused pastry with a damp cloth. Place one almond 'sausage' along the length of the oiled pastry, about 2.5 cm (1 inch) from the edge. Roll up the pastry, enclosing the almond 'sausage'. Form into a loose coil starting in the centre of an oiled 20 cm (8 inch) round loose-bottomed flan tin. Repeat with the remaining almond 'sausages' and pastry. Join one to the end of the coil in the tin, continue the coil outwards, then repeat with the last piece.

3 Beat the egg yolk with a pinch of cinnamon and brush over the top. Bake in a preheated oven, 180°C (350°F), Gas Mark 4, for 30 minutes until golden and crisp on top.

4 Remove the sides of the tin, carefully turn the coil over, return to the base of the tin and place in the oven for 10 minutes until the bottom is brown. Invert on to a cooling rack and leave to cool slightly. Sift over the icing sugar and ground cinnamon. Serve warm, cut into wedges.

Makes 12 pieces

250 g (8 oz) ground almonds

175 g (6 oz) icing sugar

1 egg, separated

few drops of almond essence

1½ tablespoons rosewater

icing sugar, for sprinkling

6 sheets filo pastry

4 tablespoons olive oil

icing sugar and ground cinnamon, to decorate

rice pudding

1 Heat the milk in a heavy, preferably non-stick saucepan. Sprinkle over the rice and bring to the boil, stirring. Lower the heat and cook very gently, stirring occasionally, until the pudding is thick, velvety and falls easily from the spoon – this may take anything up to 2 hours. Use a heat-diffusing mat, if necessary, to prevent the rice cooking too quickly and sticking. Stir in the sugar and orange flower water or rosewater to taste.

2 Pour into a serving dish or individual dishes. Serve warm or cold with pistachio nuts, almonds, and crystallized violets or roses scattered over.

Serves 4

about 1 litre (1¾ pints) milk

50 g (2 oz) short-grain pudding rice, rinsed and drained

50 g (2 oz) sugar

1–1½ tablespoons orange flower water or rosewater

chopped pistachio nuts, almonds, and crystallized violets or roses, to decorate

mint tea

Mint tea is an integral part of Moroccan hospitality. A steaming glass of the fragrant, sweet, light tea is offered as a sign of welcome, and even the poorest Moroccan feels honour-bound to offer the drink to anyone who visits their home. Mint tea may also be provided to ease delicate business negotiations. Tea arrived in Morocco in 1854 when, during the Crimean War, the blockade of the Baltic drove British merchants to seek new markets for their goods and they disposed of stocks of tea in Tangier and Mogador. The mint should be spearmint, and traditionally the sugar is cut from a sugar loaf.

2 teaspoons Chinese green tea

4 tablespons chopped mint, preferably spearmint

900 ml (1½ pints) water

sugar, to taste

To decorate:

4 lemon slices (optional)

4 small mint sprigs

1 Rinse a teapot with boiling water. Add the tea and mint to the pot. Bring the water to the boil and immediately pour into the tea pot. Leave to stand for 5 minutes.

2 Pour the tea through a strainer into warmed glasses or small cups. Add sugar to taste (remember, in Morocco tea is supposed to be very sweet) and decorate each glass or cup with a lemon slice, if liked, and a sprig of mint.

Serves 4

Variation: Iced Mint Tea
Add the sugar to the pot with the tea and mint. After steeping, pour the tea through a strainer over cracked ice so it cools quickly. Serve in cold glasses with ice cubes, decorated in the same way.

saffron tea

This tea is a speciality of the southern Moroccan town of Taliouine, the saffron capital of Morocco. The surrounding hillsides are a glorious picture for a few days when the tidy rows of the special purple crocus are in flower.

2 teaspoons Chinese green tea

1 teaspoon saffron threads

900 ml (1½ pints) water

sugar, to taste

To decorate:

4 lemon slices (optional)

4 small mint sprigs

1 Rinse a teapot with boiling water. Add the tea and saffron to the pot.

2 Bring the water to the boil and immediately pour into the tea pot. Leave to stand for 5 minutes.

3 Pour the tea through a strainer into warm glasses or small cups. Add sugar to taste and decorate each glass or cup with a lemon slice, if liked, and a mint sprig.

Serves 4